TO UNDERSTAND MA[...] WE MUST UNDERSTAND CHINA.

TO UNDERSTAND CHINA, WE MUST UNDERSTAND MAO.

This unusually sensitive and fair-minded biography allows us to grasp the many dimensions of Mao Tse-Tung: the complexities and contradictions of his character; the sweeping drama of his life and times; the far-reaching import of his actions and decisions, first as a revolutionary overturning an old order, then as a ruler creating a new one. With an epilogue written especially for this Mentor edition that offers sharp insight into the new rapprochement between China and the United States, MAO is essential reading for true understanding of one of the towering figures of our century and of one of the great nations of today.

MAO

PETER CARTER, educated at Oxford University, has been both a teacher and a writer. He is the author of four highly regarded historical novels for young people and currently lives in Birmingham, England.

MENTOR Books of Special Interest

MAO

Peter Carter

A MENTOR BOOK

NEW AMERICAN LIBRARY

TIMES MIRROR

COPYRIGHT © PETER CARTER, 1976, 1979

EPILOGUE COPYRIGHT © 1980 BY
THE NEW AMERICAN LIBRARY, INC.

The extract from the poem "Dead Water" on page 170 is taken
from *Red Candle: Selected Poems of Wen I-to,* translated by Tao
Tao Sanders, and is reprinted by kind permission of the publishers,
Jonathan Cape, Ltd.

Library of Congress Catalog Card No. 80-80843

 MENTOR TRADEMARK REG. U.S. PAT. OFF. AND FOREIGN COUNTRIES
REGISTERED TRADEMARK—MARCA REGISTRADA
HECHO EN CHICAGO, U.S.A.

SIGNET, SIGNET CLASSICS, MENTOR, PLUME, MERIDIAN AND NAL
BOOKS *are published by The New American Library, Inc.,*
1633 Broadway, New York, New York 10019

FIRST MENTOR PRINTING, JUNE, 1980

1   2   3   4   5   6   7   8   9

PRINTED IN THE UNITED STATES OF AMERICA

FOR BILL CARTER

"He presumed the Mandarins were convinced that the Centurion alone was capable of destroying the whole navigation of the port of Canton, or of any other port of China, without running the least risk from all the force the Chinese could collect."

—*Lord Anson speaking of the Governor of Canton in 1743*

"Political power grows from the barrel of a gun."

—*Mao Tse-tung in 1938*

MAO

ONE

"We can learn what we did not know."—*Mao Tse-tung*

For three thousand years China existed in a self-imposed isolation as complete as the ingenuity of an endlessly inventive nation could devise. The name it knew itself by was "The Middle Kingdom," the Kingdom at the Center of the Earth.

Around The Middle Kingdom was the rest of mankind—slothful, ignorant, seen by the Chinese as barbarians lost in darkness. Occasionally the barbarians broke into China, as the Mongols did, and the Manchus, but otherwise, throughout century after dreaming century, the people of the outer world seemed as irrelevant to China and its destiny as the rustling of leaves in a forest.

The rulers of China, the Emperors, were the Sons of Heaven—priest-kings, mediators between the remote Chinese gods and the multitudes who dwelt on China's sacred soil. On the Emperors and their ritual depended the well-being of China's people, and, less obviously, on the well-being of the Chinese depended the Emperors' continuance as rulers.

Under the Emperors the mandarins governed the land. Scholar-administrators, they were selected after a long series of competitive examinations that determined their fitness to

1

preserve order and maintain stability and to reflect in their calm observance of custom and ritual the ordered regularity of agricultural life.

From their home in China's vastness the Emperor and his mandarins looked with scorn at the world beyond their borders. What could the barbarians offer them? China was all-sufficient, not just the home of culture and civilization, but culture and civilization itself. Calm, ordered, endless, it was a symbol, for itself and for the rest of the world, of grace and elegance, of willows graceful by the riverside, of porcelain more delicate than the willow leaves, and of women more graceful and delicate than either.

But the beauty and the elegance were founded on the brute labor of millions of peasants stooped at their work in the paddy fields of the south and the wheat fields of the north. In China's fat years the backs of the peasants were broad enough to bear the cost of keeping the mandarins and the Emperor, and the cost was worth paying. China's huge and intricate system of water control, the distribution of food, the maintenance of law—all these the Emperor's servants organized, and organized well. But almost imperceptibly, as slowly as a great tree dying, China was growing poorer. The prosperous years increased the population, but the land was not increased in proportion. The peasants' land was divided and subdivided; rents increased until the farmers were in debt forever. Men found themselves living on the edge of starvation, without land, owning nothing and living by the sweat of their bodies. These men were called *koo li:* the men of bitter strength who did not live long.

But China slept. Like sleepwalkers, the Emperors conducted their rituals in the Temple of Heaven, each year plowing a symbolic furrow before the Temple that China's crops might grow. The mandarins studied the thoughts of Confucius and applied his calm precepts to their government; miracles of beauty flowered in the hands of the porcelain makers; and each year the poor grew poorer; the gap between themselves and their elegant rulers grew wider. Lost in a complacent slumber, China slept deeper.

But the outside world was not sleeping. The despised barbarians of the West, freed from the ordered round of agriculture, freed from tradition, freed, too, perhaps, from grace, mastered the technology of steam and iron. Mankind's dominion of the world had begun, but still China slumbered, dreaming of willows by the riverside, while Europes' furnaces cast their red glow across China's skies.

Already, like an uneasy dream before waking, China had heard the West. In 1742 the British seaman, George Anson, had sailed into Canton in search of supplies and repairs. The Chinese were reluctant to help, and Anson threatened to destroy Canton, the greatest port in the East. Around him was the most populous nation on earth. He had one ship and two hundred men and boys, but Anson pointed his guns at the millions, and China capitulated.

What could China do? For hundreds of years she had given ideas to the West but disdained to receive any in return. Now she was helpless before the guns of Europe. But not only the guns cowed her. The Industrial Revolution was altering the minds of those who lived in Europe. Anson's self-confidence sprang from a turmoil of change, a change that destroyed an ancient network of social relations that had stressed interdependency and replaced it with the idea of individual responsibility. This idea, which was itself the product of profound changes in the techniques of production, gave the men of the West, even the meanest of them, enormous confidence and vitality, the stronger because it was backed by guns. The men themselves were the symbols and the product of the explosive power of the society that produced them.

China and the West had traded for a thousand years, but in the eighteenth century the pace quickened. Year after year ships sailed to China. They sought trade, the traditional articles Europe had bought: tea, silk, spice, lacquer, procelain. As the West, which paid for its trade in gold, increased its manufacturing power, it looked for markets in which it could sell as well as buy. But Europe could offer little of interest to the Chinese. With a limitless supply of cheap labor, technology was unnecessary, science was brushed aside as irrelevant to China's needs, and the Chinese peasants had no interest in pots and pans, cotton shirts, or brass bedsteads. The Chinese market, which appeared so vast, was an illusion. China provided for its own needs. Before it could become a receptacle for Western goods, a demand would have to be created, and to create the demand would mean altering the very basis of Chinese society. That alteration was to come, but in a way undreamed of by either Chinese or Westerners.

In 1839 British merchants, looking for something—any-thing—they could sell in China, decided to import opium, then barely known or used in China, and forbidden by im-perial edict. The Chinese government refused to allow the sale, and the merchants provoked a war.

The conflict was brief. The Emperor turned from his ritual, the mandarins from their study of Confucius and porcelain; peasant armies, brave but ill-armed and ineptly led, fought briefly and suffered a disastrous defeat.

The defeat struck heavily at the self-confidence of China. The Heavenly Kingdom could not protect itself from foreign attack, and so what was the meaning of the Emperor and his rites at the Temple of Heaven? And what was the significance of the Confucian concept of order and harmony? Men began to question the basis of Chinese life and, perhaps for the first time in her history, began to look beyond China's borders for the answers to their questions.

The Empire trembled, but it did not fall. It lay somnolent, torpid, carried along by the inertia of centuries. The ripples of discontent as yet lapped only at the edge of Chinese life. In the vast hinterland the peasants still labored in the fields at the ever-recurring cycle of the rural year, and the slow tread of water buffalo marked the passage of the hours, and the days, and the years.

But the West was quickening its pace. In the nineteenth century the great powers—Britain, France, Germany, Russia, the United States—divided Africa and Asia among them-selves, and in their conquest of the world met in China.

In 1860 Russia took Eastern Siberia, and two years later France invaded Indo-China, both ancient dependencies of The Middle Kingdom. The attacks were further blows at the authority of the Emperor inside China. Every assault meant that the news of his helplessness was carried deeper into the heartland of his domain. The mandarins, who derived their power from him, found it increasingly difficult to exercise their authority. The elaborate techniques of water control and food distribution, worked out over millennia, no longer oper-ated smoothly. China's twin curse of flood and famine be-came more frequent, and China's poor poorer and more desperate.

All power came from the Emperor, but, as he was shown to be powerless, new leaders arose, ready to fulfill his Heavenly Role. In 1850 a failed scholar, Hung Hsiu-ch'uan, read a Bible and saw in its visions his visions, and heard in its prophecies a call to himself to bring a second Kingdom of Perfection to this earth.

Such visionaries are commonplace in any society. In societies under stress they are listened to. Hitler was heard in the misery and chaos of Germany; Hung was heard in China. His Taiping, the Great Peaceful Heavenly Rebellion, stirred tens of millions of desperate men. He gained control of much of south China, established in Nanking a government which lasted from 1853 to 1864, and almost captured the imperial capital of Peking itself.

Had Hung received support from the Western powers, or had they merely remained neutral, it is possible that he could have overthrown the ruling Manchu dynasty and founded a new dynasty of his own. But the West had no desire to see China ruled by a strong man, even a Christian strong man. Such a leader might fight off his helpers. And so the Christian nations of the West turned away from the Christian of the East, propped up the Manchus, and turned aside as Hung and his peasant armies were destroyed. In 1864 Hung, the Bible reader, committed suicide.

And now, with the Manchu Empire exhausted, discredited, and under its control, the West struck at China in earnest. Concession after concession was wrung from her. The Chinese excise was under European control, Western traders had special privileges, and large areas of Chinese cities were declared to be outside the jurisdiction of the Emperor. In 1883 Britain took Burma form the Empire. France expanded her influence in Indo-China. Russia and Germany joined in the grab. In 1900, after the secret society of the Harmonious Fists, known as the Boxers, had attacked the foreign concessions in the cities, a combined Western army took the capital, Peking, and looted the palaces of the Emperors.

But the most bitter blow of all took place in 1894. The Japanese, long despised as mere copiers of Chinese culture, attacked Korea and with contemptuous ease brushed aside the Emperor's armies there.

And at this time, into a China rotting from within and attacked from without, and under the rule of a government powerful only to do harm, Mao Tse-tung was born.

TWO

Mao was born in southwest China, in Shaoshan village in the province of Hunan. To the north the Yangtze River curves across the rice bowl of northern Hunan, itself a monument to the labor of uncounted generations; to the south rise tangled mountains, bandit-haunted then, wild and lawless, a challenge and a threat to the patient labor of the plains.

Mao's father, Mao Shun-sheng, was a peasant, owning his own land. From poor parents himself, he had been forced by poverty to join the army when young. On his return to civilian life he managed to regain the family land, and by the time Mao was born, on December 26, 1893, the family—father, mother, grandfather, Mao, and later on Mao's brothers, Mao Tse-t'an, Mao Tse-min, and his sister Mao Tse-hung—was living in what were, by Chinese standards, comfortable circumstances. By this time Mao Shun-sheng had twenty acres of land. Most Chinese who had land at all were glad to wring a living from five.

Mao Shun-sheng was a typical peasant and would have been at home wherever men have to live on the soil. He was harsh, grasping, tyrannical, and shrewd in his own way. This is obvious from the way he built up his prosperity. Raising a minute amount of capital by hard work, he bought grain from the poorer peasants and took it to the city, where he sold it for a higher price. It is the technique of the middleman and, although simple, it calls for certain virtues: patience, foresight, daring—for there is an element of risk—and practicality, the ability to weigh realistically the chances of success or failure. These are not negligible virtues, and, applied to bigger affairs, they have altered the destinies of nations. Cromwell had them, as did Lincoln, and Mao Tse-tung.

In peasant communities everyone works, except perhaps the landlord. To survive, agricultural communities must win a surplus from each harvest that will carry them through the winter and provide the seed for next year's crop. The winning of that surplus has been the struggle of the greater part of mankind during most of history. No hands, young or old, weak or strong, can be left idle in the getting of those precious extra grains, and Mao, like every other being in his village, served his apprenticeship among the paddies.

The labor in the rice fields, still to be seen across the East, is one of the most moving sights on earth—men, women, children, under straw cloaks and hats, half-naked in the tepid rain, moving slowly across the flooded fields, bent double at the backbreaking work of planting and harvesting.

As one clanks through the paddies on the slow-moving trains, the peasants look up briefly and return to their labors, unchanging through the ages. Yet change does take place, and the train that slowly crosses the rice fields, and the big jets that sketch their silver lines across the sky are portents of that change. The train clanks through the paddies, and the peasants, looking up, wonder where the train is from and where it is going and who those passengers might be who look down on them, the primary producers of the world. Mao Tse-tung had waded knee-deep through the mud of the paddies. He, above all others, saw that the peasants were ready to look up and see a new life before them.

But Mao was not bound to the rice fields. When he was eight, his father, knowing perfectly well the financial value of education, sent him to the local primary school. The curriculum in the schools of China was largely the study of the precepts of Confucius, the scholar who, in the fourth century B.C., had laid down the concepts of order and authority, and the mutual interdependence of ruler and ruled, which had served as the basis of Chinese society for two thousand years.

Confucianism had served China well, but its day was passing. Its structure of ideas, firm but supple enough to last for centuries, had been shattered by the fire power of the West. Still, the children of China sat in their clay classrooms, laboring to understand a social order that was already passing away.

The literature of Confucianism is the literature of the rice plain: of order, discipline, and work. But there is another literature in China: the literature of the mountains—of banditry, of lawlessness, of revolt. These tales were the favorites of most young Chinese, Mao included.

Tales of rebellion are always popular among the weak and the oppressed, and since all children are weak and, from their point of view, oppressed by the adult world, they turn to heroes of rebellion, such as Robin Hood, to reassure themselves of their worth and power when these are most in doubt. If this is so in the West, it is easy to see the appeal such tales have in a strict authoritarian society such as China, where fathers were invariably stern. For Mao, however, the tales were to have a lasting and serious effect, and he was to live to turn the tales of rebels in the mountains into realities in his own life.

Mao's father was heavy-handed, and so, too, was his teacher, a man who belonged to what was known as the "stern treatment" school. Harassed at home and at school, and no doubt inspired by his outlaw tales, Mao at the age of ten did what many a boy has done before and since—he ran away. Under the impression that he was heading for a nearby town, he wandered among the foothills outside Shaoshan until his father found him.

This, the first of Mao's rebellions, had some effect. He was treated more leniently both at home and at school. Probably both his rulers were shocked by the result of their treatment; after all, it is rare to find men who actually wish harm to their charges. It is just as possible, though, that old Shunsheng, who seems to have had a quirky respect for determination, recognized in his son a stubbornness that matched his own.

But if school was hard and his father severe, in his mother, Wen Ch'i-mei, Mao had a friend and an ally. She was a Buddhist, and in a simple and unaffected way she lived up to the teaching of her gentle and tolerant religion. In the house she was a moderating influence, defending the children but refusing to allow any insolence or open defiance toward their father. In strict accordance with the noble principles of her religion, Wen Ch'i-mei pitied the poor and fed them—although secretly, since old Mao was a ferocious skinflint. There can be no doubt that the example of his mother was a valuable counterweight to the father in Mao's youthful experience.

At this time Mao, too, was a Buddhist and made his devotions daily before the bronze Buddha which, on a polished table, smiled its ambiguous smile at the family. During these childhood years Mao, with his mother, made repeated attempts to convert his father, who was skeptical about religion. Later, after an alarming encounter with a tiger, Mao Shun-sheng became more sympathetic to the gods and made sacrifices before them. But it is interesting that at this time, when he was becoming religious and Mao himself was growing more skeptical, the father made no attempt to influence his son or interfere with his beliefs.

The conflict between his parents continued throughout Mao's childhood. Such parental clashes can raise acute problems for children. Their silent miseries can result in lasting wounds. When he has grown into adulthood, the person caught in parental conflicts may find himself confused over his own role, and this confusion may trigger serious psychological problems. On the other hand, the conflict can harden character, tempering it as a smith tempers steel by subjecting it to extremes of heat and cold.

In the West, where childhood is long and children pampered, weakness is often the result, but in the East, where hardship and want stand forever at the door, a child is likely to be toughened rather than weakened, for toughness is the condition of survival.

Mao was certainly made harder. As he grew older and the differences between himself and his father grew sharper and his mother's restraining hand weaker, he became increasingly bold and more sophisticated in his defense. Accused of laziness by his father, he quoted Confucius, saying that the father's role was to be kind and caring. Accused of rebellion, he quoted again, answering that the father, being bigger, should work harder than the children. But more dramatic scenes took place. Mao's father once berated him for idleness before a group of elders. Mao was furious, cursed his father in return, and ran off to a nearby lake. Mao Shun-sheng,

Wen Ch'i-mei, and the guests ran after him, but Mao climbed
a rock and threatened to jump into the lake if they came any
nearer. Although serious enough for those taking part, it is a
comical situation: a dark evening by a chilly lake, a determined boy, a furious father, a tearful mother, and a circle of
guests—without doubt more amused than fearful, but careful
to keep solemn faces.

In the end a compromise was reached. Mao's father agreed
not to beat Mao if he gave the kowtow, the traditional act of
submission made by kneeling and placing one's head in the
dust. Even at this Mao balked and insisted that he would
kneel only on one knee. This was accepted and the little
drama ended.

The incident is of interest for various reasons. It shows
Mao's growing resolution, and it illustrates something not altogether disagreeable about the father. It could not have been
easy for him to agree publicly to his son's demands, and
many a man would have rapidly altered the terms of the ar-
mistice once he returned home. But Mao Shun-sheng kept his
word.

It is also interesting to speculate further on Mao's action. It
is perfectly explicable in ordinary human terms, and such
scenes take place at all times and in all societies. But in
China, where respect for the elder was a prime virtue, it was
probably rarer than anywhere else on earth. And if the Emperor, the source and guarantee of all authority, was seen to
be powerless, then from where could any man derive his authority? The shaking of Chinese power at its source had sent
tremors through every level of society—through the court,
through the universities, through the army, down to the most
remote provinces, to the most obscure villages, to the humblest
boy. In fact, in rebelling against his father's authority, Mao,
the boy, was at one with the foremost thinkers of his time,
and the father was identified with the collapsed and ruined
Empire.

Not long after the incident at the lake, when Mao was
about thirteen, he left the primary school. As a mark of this
step into responsibility his father had the boy married to a
woman who was eight years older. This was not a real marriage, for Mao never lived with his bride; it was designed
rather as an alliance of two landowning families. More to the
point was that Mao now did full-time labor on the farm.

During the day he did a man's work, but at night he kept up his reading. He did not, however, read the Confucian classics. Mao was still enthralled by tales of romance and banditry, although, like many a boy before him, he had to read them secretly. But it was not reading only novels. Drifting across China were books and pamphlets that discussed the plight of the Empire. One of these, *Words of Warning*, came into Mao's hands. Printed in one of the great cities—Shanghai or Peking or Canton—and sent, perhaps, by junk down the vast waters of the Yangtze River, carried by mule or man, such books were exchanged from hand to hand, finally reaching young and old in China's million villages, including Shaoshan.

Words of Warning spoke of the dangers facing China and argued that the Empire needed to reform itself on a technical basis. It argued that China needed modern schools, factories, railways, and a reformed political system modeled on the Western democracies.

The book had been prompted by a feeble attempt at reform by the Emperor Kuang Hsü, who in a burst of activity known as the Hundred Days had tried to bring in some reforms in education and law. This was an attempt to match the reforms, more ruthless and more sweeping, that had helped to make Japan a major power. But Kuang's reforms were too little and too late. Not only were they inadequate to deal with China's problems, but they aroused the wrath of the Emperor's aunt, the Dowager Empress Tz'u-hsi, who imprisoned her nephew and, ruling in his stead, repealed the reforms.

Reading *Words of Warning* stimulated Mao into a desire to further his education, to relate the experience of his life, short though it was, to a broader understanding of his country's problems. And as his curiosity was being sharpened, so his experience was being widened. Famine came to Hunan, and in Changsha, the capital of the province, the poor were starving. There was grain available, but it was being hoarded by the merchants. The poor demanded that the grain be distributed, and there were severe disturbances, which were ruthlessly repressed; the leaders of the disturbances were executed. The episode was talked about a great deal in Shaoshan.

Obviously it was an exciting local event, but Mao claimed that it affected him in a deeper way. He saw the "rioters" not as rebels or mischief makers but as ordinary men driven to action by the force of circumstances, and he saw that what drove them to protest—and to die—could drive any man. In other words, he saw that external, or objective, circumstances can be decisive in one's life.

As the famine spread, so did the unrest. In Shaoshan the poor villagers seized rice from the well-off farmers, including Mao's father. Although Mao thought that this action was wrong, he sympathized with the men. It was what any men, faced with hunger, might do.

Other events were taking place in Hunan. In 1906 a huge rebellion against the imperial family had taken place on the border with Hupeh, and its echoes had not died away. The rebellion had been led by one of China's many secret socie-ites, the Ke Lao Hui, which was especially strong among the peasants. The Ke Lao Hui had a dispute with a local land-owner. The landowner took the society to court and won the decision. The Ke Lao Hui refused to accept the decision and, faced with troops, took to the mountains and raised the ban-ner of revolt. The leaders of the revolt were the heroes of the young men of Shaoshan, Mao included. It is easy to see why. The bandit heroes of the romantic tales had come to life. It was as if Robin Hood had reappeared in Sherwood Forest.

These events were not merely local; they were the products of the decay of China. Food shortages need not mean famine unless the means of distribution have broken down, and the interests of rulers and ruled need not clash unless injustice is manifest. The causes of China's trouble are clearer to us now than they were to many Chinese then, but every Chinese knew that his country was in serious difficulty. Mao remem-bered reading a pamphlet on the West's attacks on China, which began with the words, "Alas, China will be sub-jugated," and feeling depressed.

Depression, however, was not the answer to China's prob-lems or to the more pressing question of Mao's own future. Now sixteen, he was dissatisfied with the narrowness of life in a Chinese village and was looking for horizons not bounded by the dikes of the rice fields. But where was the new life to be found? For a time Mao left home and lived with a law student, reading the Chinese classics in a desultory fashion with an old scholar who lived in Shaoshan. But he also read anything else that came his way.

During these months Mao was not reading anything systematically, although that is not the same thing as saying that his studies were unfruitful. It is probable that Mao needed the apparent idleness to allow his mind the random speculation that would enable it to flower fully. This kind of apparently purposeless reading and lounging, which seems futile to conventional minds, is often the prelude to action on a huge scale, whether in the arts or politics or any other activity. It appears to be related to a form of delayed maturity, as if some creative people needed a prolonged adolescence so that when maturity comes it will be fuller. Mao was to infuriate his father for years to come with seemingly immature behavior, but when his maturity was upon him, he was to shake the world.

It was not to be expected that old Mao would allow his son to dawdle away his time indefinitely, and the father decided to apprentice him to a rice merchant. Mao was not opposed to this, thinking that the job would be interesting, but at this time he heard of a school in the nearby town of Tungshan which offered modern subjects as well as the traditional Chinese curriculum. Such schools were springing up all over China, following the example of the Christian missionary schools. Mao Shun-sheng was opposed to his son's attending the school, but after friends had urged on him the advantages of a modern education, and after Mao had actually borrowed money to finance himself, he reluctantly agreed. Mao left Shaoshan for the first time in his life and turned to face the outside world.

When the young Mao, at the age of sixteen, took his first step in his long march into history, he was tall and strong and toughened by hard work. He was also rough in manners and speech, stubborn, moody, restless, with no apparent outstanding ability, no particular talent. He was merely a youth with a certain sympathy for his fellow men and a strong mind he had yet to learn how to use. What was to become of him depended not only on himself but on the environment in which he was to find himself and where he would learn to be himself. If he had been born in a different country—in Britain, say, or America—he might have become a builder or a shopkeeper, perhaps a labor leader. But he was born in a China itself struggling to be reborn, where all old categories of thought and life were being destroyed and where character and resolution were to be of more importance than birth, breeding, or money. And character and resolution Mao had in plenty—enough to change the world.

THREE

The Tungshan Academy had been built in the shadow of a graceful, conical hill, where the bells of a white pagoda tinkled in the wind. The school itself had a more forbidding look. It was surrounded by a high wall the pupils called the Great Wall of China, but its severity was softened by a chain of pools where fish drifted slowly through the weeds. Mao had some doubt as to whether he would be accepted by the academy, but as it was in his mother's home district, he was allowed in without too much trouble—although the principal raised his eyebrows on hearing Mao's age, which was considerably above that of his other pupils.

Being accepted, Mao settled down to work, but the first lesson he learned was an unpleasant and surprising one: he was disliked. The rest of the pupils, many of whom were mere children, found the sight of the tall Mao among them ridiculous, and they let him know their feelings. The school was divided into three gangs, each based on one of the divisions of the district. As an outsider Mao belonged to none of these gangs and, belonging to none, was hated by all. In addition to this, most of the pupils were the sons of wealthy men and came from a class with which Mao had had little contact. With his peasant slouch and rough clothes he was the butt for the contemptuous snobbery of the elegant youths who wandered through the school in expensive gowns.

15

Isolated and disliked, Mao went through a period of depression, but now the toughness of his character began to show. He worked hard, impressing his masters with his ability. Oddly enough, for one who had been attracted to the school because of its modern curriculum, he did best at the Chinese classics, the study of the ancient masters of Chinese literature and thought. His study of these writers then led him on to think about the nature of the rulers of China, and four Emperors particularly impressed him.

The first two of these were the semi-mythical Yao and Shun, who were credited with the system of flood control that first made, and still makes, life in China possible. The third was Ch'in Shih Huang Ti, who had built the Great Wall, thus securing China's only vulnerable border. The fourth was the peasant, Han Wuh-ti, who had founded the mighty Han dynasty, which had laid down the foundations of Chinese life.

It is impossible not to think of Mao, as he slouched through the streets of Tungshan, laughed at and mocked, without believing that he comforted himself with the knowledge that the greatest of Chinese ruling lines had been laid down by one such as himself, a peasant, a man of the fields, and, for all his faults, a man of the people.

But as the weeks passed Mao found among his fellow scholars young men whom he liked and who liked him, and his life became more tolerable. Classes over, he and his friends would walk to the fish ponds and talk of the happenings of their own small world, and also of the events of the greater world beyond them.

One of their topics was perpetually on the lips of every thinking Chinese: the plight of China. Could their country be made strong again? The question was given urgency not only by the attacks on China but by the example of the Island Kingdom to the east—by Japan.

Like China, Japan had isolated herself from the outside world and for centuries had maintained herself in secrecy—a medieval mystery, barely known, scarcely understood, lost in the vast moat of the North Pacific. And in eighty years, under a ruthless and determined leadership, she had built a modern power base of her own and had burst upon an astonished world, cracking her whip over China, humiliating the vast Russian Empire, and, most satisfying of all, signing a treaty as an equal with Britain, the most formidable of the imperial powers.

A stream of Chinese had gone to Japan to study her institutions. On their return they were to be found across China, even in towns as petty as Tungshan. One such taught in the academy. He was called the "False Foreign Devil," "false" because, although he cut off his queue (the pigtail all Chinese were forced to wear by the Manchu rulers), his courage had failed him and he wore an artificial one. "Foreign devil" because his appearance looked foreign and all foreigners were devils to the Chinese.

Although this man was despised, it was from him that Mao learned of the strength of the Japanese Empire. That was enough. The battle could be won by the East—if not by Japan, then by China.

And so China could become great again. But how? Mao believed that all that was needed were a few reforms such as had been tried, ineffectually, by the Emperor before his mother had imprisoned him. But now the Dowager Empress, who was undoubtedly a wicked woman, was dead, and Mao thought that the new Emperor, or rather his Regent, for the Emperor was a child, was a good man. He, with his advisers, would redeem China. All would be well with these good men ruling the Empire.

This was not an idea unique to Mao. Chinese society taught its members to look for good men in the running of its affairs. It was the lesson Confucius taught, and in relation to the China of the past it was not incorrect. China was an agrarian society, and, like other agrarian states, its problems had been, in fact, simple: either enough food was grown or it was not. Apart from increasing land area, such a society has no technique for increasing crop yield; the problem it faces is always one of food distribution. A good ruler may see that food is distributed, a bad one may not. Consequently, rural states do depend on good men for their proper working. Oddly enough, in highly industrialized societies the same answer is often advocated. The problems there can seem so complicated that they appear insuperable by democratic means, and the citizens in desperation may turn to supermen to help them—men they believe strong enough to deal with the problems and good enough not to misuse the power they are given. The fallacy of this belief may be seen in the careers of Hitler and Stalin.

The desire for a hero is strong in immature minds, and it is not surprising that Mao now added to his bandit heroes other men he could admire. One of the books he read in Tungshan was titled *Great Heroes of the World*. This might, with more accuracy, have been called *Great Heroes of the Western World*, since the great men were all Westerners, but Mao read it with interest. It is fascinating to observe that the two figures who most impressed him were George Washington and Napoleon: the first a man who, against all odds, led his country to freedom after years of war; the second, one who altered the face and life of Europe by releasing the revolutionary fervor of its peoples—and both, of course, were great soldiers.

Many other Chinese pined, as Mao did, for a hero. As yet, the complexity of the problem of national regeneration was barely understood even by the leading thinkers of China, let alone by a schoolboy. But the understanding was to come, both to Mao and to China, in lessons as bitter as those any nation has ever had to learn.

But now Mao was growing restless. The academy, which had seemed to promise so much, offered less than he wanted. He began to think of going to Changsha, the provincial capital of Hunan. Mao had heard of the splendors of the city, and also of its schools, which were reputed to be excellent. He persuaded a master at his school to give him a letter of introduction, and in the spring of 1911 he left Tungshan and its tranquil fish ponds, left the white pagoda and its windstirred bells, and took a steamer down the river to the city where his life was to be transformed in the crucibles of revolution and civil war.

FOUR

The journey to Changsha was the second longest Mao had taken in his life, and like the trip to Tungshan, it was a gamble. There was no guarantee that he would gain admission to a school or, if he did, that he would be successful, for as yet he had not been tested against serious standards. But he was about to be.

In moving to Changsha, Mao was entering a world as different from Tungshan as Tungshan had been from Shaoshan. Changsha was a real city, the capital of a province of twenty million people. It was the natural focus for the intellectual life of the area, and it presented, as all major cities do, the conflicts of the region in a sharpened form. Hunan itself had always been noted for the fiery quality of its people, and Changsha was a revolutionary hotbed. As well as drawing on the resources of its own region, the city was in touch with the outside world, which for Mao was still only an idea, for it is worth noting that as yet, at seventeen, Mao had not seen a map of the world.

Changsha was on the railway that linked it with the huge port of Canton to the south and the imperial capital of Peking in the north. Steamers connected it with the Yangtze River, which was a major route to Shanghai, the bastion of the imperial powers whose gunboats chugged up and down the river to within a few score miles of Changsha itself. If

Mao had any qualities other than peasant stubbornness, it was in this city that they would be tested.

The Higher Primary School took pupils from Mao's district as a matter of course, so Mao entered the school without difficulty and settled down to his new life. But one of the things he read outside school was of more significance than any book he read inside it, because for the first time in his life he read a newspaper.

The paper was no ordinary one. Called the *Min-lin-pao*, the *People's Strength*, it was controlled by a group of exiles who believed that only a national revolution and the end of the monarchy would save China.

The exiles and their supporters inside China were banded together in a secret society known as the T'ung-meng Hui, or the Alliance Party. China had many secret societies, some of them criminal, such as the Green Gang in Shanghai, some of them merely trade organizations or workers' unions, but many of them deeply involved in politics, as the Society of Harmonious Fists had been in the Boxer Rebellion.

Of all the secret societies in China at that time the T'ung-meng Hui was the most significant. It was well organized, had a clear political aim—the establishment of a democratic system of government—and it was led by one of the great names in Chinese history, Dr. Sun Yat-sen (1866–1925).

Dr. Sun was a Christian convert who had been trained as a doctor by Americans. For years he was actually an American citizen but had retained close contact with Chinese affairs. He had founded the Alliance Party to unite all the anti-monarchical parties inside China, and his followers, who penetrated the army and the government, were already preparing the blow that was finally to bring down the Manchus. The *People's Strength* was Sun's paper, and when Mao read it, two future leaders of China—the learned cosmopolitan doctor and the rough country boy—touched hands briefly across a gulf of time and space and culture.

What Mao read in the paper was dramatic news. In Canton, to the south, the military leader of the Alliance Party, Hsuan Hsing, had led an armed rebellion. The uprising had failed and its leaders had been executed, but the revolt awoke in many Chinese patriots revolutionary feelings that were to simmer throughout the summer until, in October, a greater rebellion broke out.

Mao was deeply moved by the account of the Canton revolt and the martyrdom of its leaders. He wrote an article demanding a republic and pasted it on the school wall. A few months previously Mao had been arguing that a "good" emperor would save China. Now nothing would satisfy him but that there should be no emperor at all and that democracy was the only answer to China's ills. Mao's ideas were obviously confused, but confusion was the air every Chinese breathed in those troubled times.

Mao was not alone in his sudden passion for an end to the Manchus. A group of students vowed to cut off their queues as a gesture of defiance against the monarchy. Mao and a friend cut theirs off but then found that their comrades had had second thoughts, as many another revolutionary has had when the time came to translate words into deeds. Mao flexed his muscles and forcibly removed the queues of the unwilling students.

These actions were rough and immature, but they show an aspect of Mao's personality that was to become of great importance: his readiness to take decisive action and, if necessary, to use force. This is not, of course, pleasant or easily defensible, but it shows a powerful self-confidence, which is the prime quality in a leader.

In 1911 Mao's actions were without significance, except as they were typical of the mood of young China. Other men were in the center of the stage, and mightier events were taking place there. In October, just six months after Mao arrived in Changsha, the long-awaited revolution started.

The revolution exploded quite literally. On October 10, in the army headquarters in Hankow, a bomb blew up. The authorities investigated and uncovered a revolutionary plot among a group of young officers. The men, who were members of the T'ung-meng Hui, were executed, but the ax was no longer sufficient to defend the monarchy. The officer corps was too strongly influenced by Sun Yat-sen. The day after the officers of Hankow were put to death, the garrison of Huchang, just across the river, also revolted, and this time the authorities were powerless to prevent it.

The Huchang rebellion was the signal for a general uprising across the whole of south China. City after city, province after province delcared for a republic, and before the wave of popular feeling, the armies of the Manchus were washed away.

Within a month most of China south of the Yangtze was in the hands of the Republicans. Here and there, cities, like Changsha, held out, but the success of the revolution seemed assured. What was not so clear at the time was that in the north, where the Manchu influence was strongest, the imperial army under the command of the Emperor's chief of staff, Yuan Shih-k'ai, was holding its ground.

Changsha, too, was holding out. The governor had declared martial law, and his guns controlled the streets. But emissaries of the revolution were active in the city, and the white banners of the Alliance Party fluttered over the rooftops. In the schools propagandists were busy asking for volunteers to join the Republican army, which was at Hankow. Mao promptly volunteered, but he had heard that the streets of Hankow were very wet and so, in his practical and matter-of-fact way, he decided to borrow a pair of serviceable shoes before he went. He had a friend, a member of one of the imperial troops camped outside the city, who, he thought, would lend him the shoes, but as he went to get them, Mao was stopped by sentries and detained. While he was being held, without assistance from him, Changsha fell.

Although Mao remembered a battle outside the wall of the city, its fall was not dramatic. Under the influence of the T'ung-meng Hui, the infantry brigade guarding it delcared for the revolution. They marched to the gates, fired a few volleys in the air, the gates opened, and Changsha was part of the new China. The governor, stronger in common sense than valor, escaped through a hole in the wall, which he had prudently prepared against such a day.

And so, bloodlessly and sensibly, the revolution had come to Changsha. But within weeks blood in plenty was spilled. The leaders of the revolutionary forces inside the city, Chiao Ta-feng and Ch'en Tso-hsin, had been members of the T'ung-meng Hui. Both men thought that the revolution should bring tangible rewards to the poor people of the city, and they were ready to see that they got them. Alarmed by their attitude, the landowners and businessmen called in a "strong man," T'an Yen-k'ai. He was declared governor and promptly had Ch'en and Chiao shot and their bodies thrown into the street, where Mao saw them. The same scenes were taking place across China. The men of power, having, as they thought, achieved their ends, were making it clear that any belief in the redistribution of wealth was one better not advocated.

But as the excitement of the first weeks of the insurrection died away, it became clear that the revolution was not over. Yuan Shih-k'ai and his troops across the Yangtze were by no means defeated, and it was beginning to look as if China might be entering a civil war on a vast and bloody scale, only to end divided between north and south.

Again the revolutionaries called for volunteers for the army, and again Mao answered the call. At first he considered joining a militia force raised from among the students, but instead he joined the regular army and became Private Mao.

Mao's motives in joining the army are clear: "I wanted to see the revolution succeed," he said. What he had seen of the murder of Chiao and Ch'en had impressed him and may have given him the first lesson in power: that holding power is as important as gaining it. It is certain that at this time Mao had no desire to become a revolutionary leader himself. Indeed, a friend of his at the time has said that he had the typical peasant's contempt for disorder, but it seemed likely that China was in for a long period of struggle and that vast and immeasurable changes might take place. An astute man might well sense that experience in the real army could be of value in the years to come. But apart from speculation, Mao found the students' corps confused and ill-organized—features firmly in the tradition of student protest movements—and was not prepared to waste his time in it.

So at the age of eighteen Mao found himself a soldier of the revolution and under the command of T'an Yen-k'ai, who had shot the original leaders of the rebellion in Changsha.

The fisrt military lesson Mao learned was the one all soldiers have to learn: how to wait. For six months his regiment dawdled under the walls of Changsha as the Republican forces and the army of the Emperor marshaled themselves for the coming war. Mao drilled, did small tasks for the officers, and read a great deal. Interestingly enough, although Mao was never one for standing on his dignity, at this time he was sufficiently concerned about his status as a student not to draw his own water from the wells but to pay a water carrier to bring it, although this meant spending a considerable sum from his minuscule wage. Mao was not impressed by his fellow soldiers, whom he thought a miserable collection of men, but he met two he admired—a miner and a blacksmith. These were the first men Mao had met from what might be called the industrial working class, and meeting them meant that Mao had significantly widened his social horizon. These fresh contacts came as Mao made another discovery. In a magazine given to him by an officer he came, for the first time, across the word "socialism."

But Mao was not to pursue new interests while he was in the army, for his military career came to an abrupt end. In the summer of 1912 Sun Yat-sen, who was Provisional President of the even more provisional Republic, made an astonishing gesture. Anxious to avoid the horrors of civil war and conscious that his party was running out of money, he offered the Presidency to Yuan Shih-k'ai if Yuan would ensure the abdication of the Manchu Emperor.

Although it meant betraying his master, Yuan was perfectly ready to accept these terms. He promptly arranged for the Emperor to retire and assumed the title of President. To the Chinese it now seemed that the revolution had succeeded. The Empire was now a Republic, a parliament was to be founded, and the all-important unity of China had been maintained. Believing this to be the case, Mao left the army and returned to civilian life. But if he thought that China's problem had been solved, he was now face to face with a more pressing one—that of his own future.

FIVE

The next months were a period of drift for Mao. He had been unsettled by his time in the army, and the Higher Primary School did not inspire him. The curriculum was too restricted and he found the regulations petty and restrictive. Millions of young Chinese were going through the same experience. The revolution, with its shattering of old institutions, had made them highly critical of traditional Chinese life. After all, China was to be re-created, the old swept away, and a new China built. As the dragon banners of the Emperor were hauled down and the five colors of the Alliance Party run up, so, it seemed, was the China of the mandarins and of Confucius fading away.

If China was to be renewed, she would need all sorts of modern techniques, and there were plenty of sharp-eyed businessmen ready to offer training for them. The newspapers were full of advertisements for new schools that promised rapid training with the lure of immediate success. Mao spent a lot of time reading the advertisements, although he had no idea what he wanted to do or any standard for judging the schools. He applied to a police training school, but before he was enrolled he was attracted by a soap-making school. The advertisement for this pointed out that the Western powers were great—and clean. If China became clean—and it was an undeniably dirty country—then it would become great too. Mao, seeing a way both to further himself and to aid his country, was impressed and paid his entrance fee, but then met a friend who was a law student and who urged him to become a lawyer. The advertisement for the law school was even more alluring than that of the soap school, promising that all who entered would be rich and distinguished in three years.

What old Mao Shun-sheng thought about his son's leaping from plan to plan may be easily guessed at; certainly it is not hard to imagine his feelings when Mao wrote home and said that he would not study law, after all, but had decided to become an economist. Mao had met another friend who had said that China would need economists more than lawyers. Mao enrolled in a private college, but even this was not his last stop, for reading yet another advertisement, he signed up for a course at a government school instead. This time Mao Shun-sheng was not displeased. He was sharp enough to see the advantages of a grounding in economics, and he gave his approval to Mao's new career—which lasted for four weeks.

The trouble was that the course in the school was conducted in English, and Mao scarcely knew the alphabet. Consequently, the lessons were incomprehensible to him, and he was forced to withdraw. However, undaunted, he joined another school, the Changsha First Middle School. This was large and well run, but its curriculum was too closely linked to the old learning for Mao's taste, and its regulations had been designed for a different age. Mao found both the lessons and the regulations irritating, so he left that school, too.

Mao's predicament is not without humor. He had tried, if halfheartedly, both the old and the new learning, and both had failed to satisfy him. Now he faced the future unprepared for anything.

What he did next was probably the most sensible thing he could have done. A public library, the first in Hunan, had recently been opened, and Mao spent the next six months studying there. The library seems to have been remarkably well stocked; Mao read Darwin, John Stuart Mill, Adam Smith, father of economics, as well as books on logic, history, and geography. Here, for the first time in his eighteen years, he saw a map of the world.

Mao was also becoming increasingly interested in socialism. Now, with more time on his hands, he was able to make a more systematic study of the ideas that were attracting the attention of many earnest thinkers in China.

Until the turn of the century the West had affected China in only the most brutal way, shattering old institutions but offering no answers to the very problems it created. But just as China was altering, so was the West. The system of unbridled capitalism that had seemed so invincible during the nineteenth century was being increasingly criticized in its own homelands. It was becoming clear that capitalism worked on a cycle of boom and slump, and, great though the benefits of capitalism had been, the slumps were becoming longer and the booms shorter. The consequence of this was prolonged unemployment, with the evil of poverty growing more severe as the years passed. In the industrial nations, particularly in Britain, France, and Germany, men were speculating on possible alternative systems, especially socialism: the belief that a just and humane society might be created if the means of production—the mines, factories, and the land—were under the control of the working class, organized in a collective state.

As the West pushed into the nonindustrial world, taking with it the capitalistic ethic of unrestrained individual freedom, there followed, as silent and as inescapable as a shadow, its enemy, socialism. And so, concepts created in distant cities, under conditions undreamed of by the peasantry of China, came to them.

As Mao grappled with these ideas in the library of Changsha, his father found out that his son was neither working nor studying in a school. Mao Shun-sheng was furious and cut off his son's allowance. During the next weeks Mao was virtually destitute, a condition he accepted with the equanimity with which he always treated physical hardship. Dressed in his jacket and trousers of coarse blue cloth, he walked the streets of Changsha, oblivious to the irony of the five banners of the Republic, which, fluttering from every building, promised "Benevolence, Wisdom, Harmony, Righteousness, and Truth." Mao subsisted on a beggar's diet of a few rice cakes a day and lived in a guild house, a semi-charitable hostel for the natives of his home district. This hostel was a rough sort of place; ex-soldiers, students, vagabonds of all types lived there, few with jobs and none with any money. Brawls were frequent, especially between the students and the soldiers, and it is a mark of Mao's levelheadedness that he, whose courage was never in doubt, kept out of these meaningless fights. In fact, during one particularly savage fracas he hid in the lavatory.

This period in Mao's life is reminiscent of the time in Shaoshan when he dropped out of school. There is apparent drift, or rather, inactivity and idleness, which hides what is really intense, as sleep disguises the creative dreamwork of a dreamer. But sleepers awake. The dream has to be related to the waking world, and Mao could not walk in his limbo forever. Even the hardiest student could not live on rice cakes alone. Mao began thinking about his future, and after deep thought he decided to become a teacher.

Once more he began to comb the advertisements, and he came across an attractive one for the Fourth Normal School of Changsha. This school, a teachers' training college, had certain real advantages. Its standards were high but the charges were low, and there was cheap accommodation. There was also a stiff entrance examination, but Mao passed it without difficulty and was entered in the school. He had just one more change to adjust to.

After a few months the Fourth Normal was amalgamated with the First Normal School. This combination was of great value to Mao. The First Normal was the best college in Hunan. It had been heavily endowed under the Emperors, and its wealth enabled it to attract teachers of the highest quality. In addition, the combined colleges had more than a thousand pupils. Among such a mass of students only scholars of genuine ability would make their mark. Mao was faced with a real test, both of his ability and his character.

A school friend of Mao's has given a picture of him as he entered the school: a tall, strong youth, slow in speech and clumsy in his movements, badly dressed, with shoes that needed mending. The rough dress was explained by Mao's lack of money, the slowness of speech was, in fact, the reserve of a thoughtful man, and the clumsiness speaks of Mao's peasant origins and is typical of the laborer who needs slow strength to do his work and to whom grace is the least of the virtues.

Clumsiness of movement, however, does not necessarily indicate clumsiness of mind, as Mao was to demonstrate. At the First Normal, as at all Chinese schools, the ability to write in the admired classical style was greatly valued. Mao was an excellent stylist and had a genuine poetic talent.

Mao's first year at college was uneventful. He disliked many of the regulations, which he thought petty and meaningless, and he found some of the academic requirements irksome, but his protest against them was more humorous than revolutionary. For instance, in drawing he drew an oval and called it "Egg," and another time he drew a semicircle over a straight line and called it "Sunset."

Even in his first year Mao's originality expressed itself. He made the acquaintance of a senior student, itself an unusual event in the caste-conscious college, and together they went on a walking holiday. That two students should take to the road was astonishing enough in China, but Mao and his friend, Siao Yu, decided to keep themselves by begging. This action was incomprehensible to the masters of the school, but the two were allowed to go. Siao Yu wanted to go on the journey in order to widen his experience, but it is doubtful that this was Mao's motive. He had plenty of experience in poverty, and a firsthand knowledge of the Chinese countryside. It seems more likely that Mao went in order to maintain his contact with the ordinary life of China, the life of the farm and the village, the teahouse and the road.

Siao Yu has left an account of his journey with Mao, and he paints a remarkably tranquil picture of life in the Chinese countryside in 1912. The reasons for this calm state are worth considering. After the agreement between Sun Yat-sen and Yuan Shih-k'ai, a truce of sorts had been patched up between the armies in the field. The parliament that Yuan had assembled in Peking, although it was a disgusting travesty of democracy, gave a semblance of order to the country. The basic stability of Chinese society reasserted itself, and the country went through a brief Indian summer.

In this pleasant atmosphere Mao returned to Changsha and continued his studies. He did this in an orderly and methodical way, impressing his fellow students with his application. He also spent a great deal of time studying world affairs. The college had a newspaper room, and Mao spent many of his evenings carefully going through the international news. Observers have often noted Mao's closeness to the peasant world, but even then he was scrupulous in his attention to the events beyond China.

Another of Mao's characteristics began to show itself at this time. In the long talks and arguments, common among students everywhere, Mao was noted for his ability to listen. When others talked he stayed silent, content to take a back seat until the topic seemed exhausted. Then he would lean forward and make a powerful and lucid summing up. This is a far more unusual ability than might at first appear, for it depends not on a quick tongue, or even on the capacity to think clearly, but on self-confidence—the readiness to wait, knowing that when one does speak, others will listen.

In 1915 Mao's growing powers were recognized by his fellow students: he was elected secretary of the Students' Society. In a school as distinguished as his this was a mark of high esteem, especially as Mao was still a junior and such a position would have been coveted by many of his seniors. In this new position Mao's radical views came to the fore. The petty rules that he had ignored during his first months in the school now came under attack from him. He organized an Association for Student Self-Government to rouse the students into opposing unreasonable school demands. But his activity was not merely obstructive. He believed that new ideas and subjects should find a place in the school curriculum, and the Students' Association was active in pressing for this.

Of course, Mao was not alone in pressing for alterations. Education, like everything else, is subject to changes in the society in which it is set, and students are among the first to detect these changes—and to respond to them. After a brief period of calm, the changes were to become increasingly severe. But to understand these changes we must leave the young Mao as he takes his first taste of power, leave the First Normal School and its ardent students, leave too, the city of Changsha, industrious beside the Hsiang River, and leave the mountains and plains of Hunan and the China in which they are set, and turn again to the grim nations of the West.

Backed by vast industries and its iron technology, the West dominated the world, and its gray warfleets ensured that dominance. But the world was paying the price for the West's supremacy. Throughout the nineteenth century the Western powers had seized huge areas of the globe, not merely countries, but continents, and used them both as sources of cheap raw materials and as markets for the increasing surplus of goods they were manufacturing.

For thirty years the system of global exploitation had worked successfully, at least for the imperialistic powers. Although minor quarrels had taken place over the spoils of Africa and Asia, these had usually been settled without too much violence. As the twentieth century dawned, however, the disputes were becoming more serious. Germany, the last of the major powers to industrialize but, in 1914, the strongest, was increasingly discontented with her part of the world's loot. Determined to get what she regarded as her fair share, she had started a massive arms program. Now her huge army threatened France, and her powerful navy threatened Britain.

Still, to most people war between the major powers was unthinkable. But forces were at work that seemed beyond men's control. Throughout the first years of the twentieth century Europe had become enmeshed in a network of treaties, each designed to prevent the dominance of any one country—particularly Germany—and to prevent war, but each, in fact, ensuring that the slightest conflict between the most minor countries would bring it about. Only one incident was required to bring about such a conflict, and in June 1914 the incident occurred.

At Sarajevo, in Bosnia, the Archduke of Austria and his wife were assassinated by a gang of terrorists who were demanding independence for Serbia. Austria demanded reparations from the Serbian government, who appealed for aid from her protector, Russia. Faced with the might of the Russian Empire, Austria turned to her ally, Germany. In her turn Russia called on France, and France on Britain. In six weeks Europe was involved in a war that was to last four years, ruin her economy, kill ten million men, and involve the whole world, from the waters of the North Atlantic to the fever-ridden forests of the Congo. The war affected the lives of every man and woman, including the secretary of the Students' Association of the First Normal School earnestly studying his books in the city of Changsha.

SIX

The war was not long in affecting China. Like her European enemies, Germany had bases in China, particularly the port of Tsingtao. In August 1914 Japan, Britain's ally in the East, declared war on Germany and promptly seized Tsingtao. China was in no position to prevent Japan's actions, but it was with bitterness that she saw a part of her territory pass from Germany to Japan.

But worse was to come. In January 1915 the Japanese government presented China with what became known as the Twenty-One Demands, which, if accepted, would have meant that China would have become Japan's vassal, a mere subject state with the control of her economy in the hands of a hostile power.

The demands were made secretly and were negotiated by Yuan Shih-k'ai, the President of the ramshackle Republic. Yuan's duty, of course, was to defend the integrity of the Republic, but he was ready to cooperate with the Japanese, for he wanted their support in carrying out a plan he had long prepared—to end the Republic and restore the Empire, with himself as Emperor.

Yuan had already taken steps to achieve this end. He had secured from the West a large loan that made him financially independent. He believed that the army, which had been his creation, would support him, and the bureaucracy, the mandarins, were not opposed to a return of the old order. All was, in fact, ready for this desirable event. The dynasty was proclaimed, the date for the enthronement of the Emperor announced, and Yuan, in what was perhaps the most optimistic act in human history, actually plowed the obligatory ritual furrow around the Temple of Heaven in Peking.

Then the Twenty-One Demands became known. A wave of real anger united the Chinese people. That they should be humiliated by the Western powers was bitter enough; that Japan should do the same thing was intolerable. The people, the army, and the mandarins turned against Yuan, and on December 25, 1915, the general commanding the army of the province of Hunan rebelled. One by one the other garrisons of China rose in revolt, and by March it was clear that Yuan's day as ruler of China was over. In June he died, and after six years of the Republic, China was left without a leader and without a government.

In fact, China was worse off than she had been. Before 1911, no matter how weak or unpopular it had been, she had had a semblance of a central government, and even under Yuan the internal cohesion of the country had been maintained. But with the overthrow of Yuan the generals realized their power. Any man who commanded an army could act as he wished. The generals set themselves up in their provinces as virtual independent rulers, as the warlords of China.

If in 1910 Mao, reading the words "China will be subjugated," had felt depressed, then he and all like him had more cause now for depression. The Peking government was now the toy of whichever general had most force at his disposal. In the south, in Canton, the genuine Republicans under Sun Yet-sen were powerless, although Sun declared an alternative government there. But even that feeble body was dependent on the protection of generals as brutal and corrupt as those of the north. "Alas, poor China" might well be the words on every patriot's lips, and despair be in every patriot's heart.

But in the dark night attempts were being made to relight the flame of China's greatness. In the cities dedicated men were looking for new answers to China's problems. One of these was the Professor of Ethics in the First Normal School, and Mao's tutor, Yang Ch'ang-chi.

Yang was a distinguished scholar and widely traveled, having studied for ten years in the West. Although well aware of the power of the Western nations, and an advocate of the modernization of China, he was deeply patriotic and had no wish to see his country become a carbon copy of Europe. Yang was also a friend of another outstanding man, Ch'en Tu-hsiu, the Dean of Letters of Peking University. Ch'en was another ardent advocate of the modernization of China, and he had founded a magazine, the *Ching-nien,* or *New Youth. New Youth,* as its name suggests, was addressed primarily to the young people of China, to those least committed to old ways of thought. Unlike Yang, Ch'en was ready to throw out lock, stock, and barrel China's traditional ways of life, stating that only "Mr. Democracy and Mr. Science" could save her. It would be hard to overestimate the influence *New Youth* had on its readers. In the chaos and decay of the Republic it gave a clear call to a new way of life.

Mao was profoundly affected by the magazine and its call for renewal, but he had already started his personal program for his own regeneration. With two friends he began a series of exercises to strengthen both his mind and body in order to make himself worthy of the task of rebuilding his country. They called themselves the "Three Heroes," a reference to three rebels in one of the romances Mao was so fond of. The Three Heroes stayed in the open, barely clothed, taking not only sun baths but rain baths, and wind baths, too. They slept in the open, sleeping indoors only when the frost drove them there, and lived on the most frugal of diets. No doubt in anticipation of a future career in politics, they also tried to strengthen their voices by shouting as loudly as they could.

Mao was also looking for acquaintances outside the school with whom he could share the renewal *New Youth* urged upon him. He put one advertisement in a Changsha newspaper, asking to meet patriotic young men who would be ready to make sacrifices for their country. He signed his advertisement "Twenty-Eight Stroke Character," after the number of brush strokes needed to make up the characters of his name. Unfortunately, not many patriotic young men read the paper he chose to advertise in, for he received only three replies— or, as Mao said, two and a half, for one of the men who answered came, listened in silence, and left. This man was called Li Li-san, and Mao and he were destined to meet again in vastly different circumstances.

Around the Three Heroes another group began to form. These were young men and women of the utmost seriousness and dedication. For them the future of China was all, and light talk and idle chatter were frowned upon. Once Mao was at the house of a friend who called in a servant to discuss the price of meat for the evening meal. Mao was so annoyed that he left and would not speak to the man again.

Telling the story in later years, Mao himself found it amusing, and to us, now, it might sound priggish. The affluent West has long been insulated against hardship, but the young people of China lived in a world where on the streets outside their doors they could see injustice, famine, and death. Well might men be serious in such a world, and well might the idealism of *New Youth* capture their imagination.

Under the influence of the magazine Mao and his friends founded a society in the First Normal School, the New People's Study Society to debate the issues Ch'en Tu-hsiu had raised. From this society came men and women who were to alter the face of China in the years to come.

While the New People's Society debated the role of Mr. Democracy and Mr. Science, it is significant that Mao had joined another society, the Ch'uan-shan Hsue-she. This was a society for the study of the thought of a famous Chinese of the seventeenth century, Wang Fu-chih, who, when the Manchus had conquered China, had refused to serve under them. The implication of this is obvious: at a time when China was under attack, Wang, himself a Hunanese, was a symbol of resistance to foreign dominance. But it is equally significant that Wang had flown in the face of all tradition by defending the most despised of all occupations in China—the soldier's.

In joining the Ch'uan-shan Hsue-she, with its concentration on a hero from China's own past, Mao was counterbalancing the stress Ch'en laid on Western answers for China's problems, and in doing this he was undoubtedly responding to his deeply patriotic feelings. It is also possible to wonder whether Mao was not equally attracted by the warlike nature of Wang, and whether the thought of war and military command was not very much present in Mao's mind then. Anyone could see that China's problems, especially the problem of the warlords, would need force to be solved. The soldier's life, the Spartan existence, the fundamental decencies of comradeship, the discipline of obedience and command, and the conflict of wills that lies behind battle—all these clearly appealed to Mao then and in the years to come, and not even his worst enemies doubted his military ability.

They did not doubt it in Changsha in 1917, either. In that year, when the ragged and savage armies of two warlords were battling for control of Hunan, Mao was elected to command the students' volunteer army that was formed to defend the school. Not lacking in self-confidence, Mao accepted the post. Not lacking in ruthlessness, either, he lined the walls with bamboo splinters inclined so as to poke out the eyes of anyone trying to climb the walls. In his defense of the school, as in all his other activities, he was not playing games.

This seriousness is shown in a story Mao's friend and admirer, Emi Siao, tells of him at this time. When discussing the role of the Chinese people in the coming struggle, Mao said, "There are two kinds of people in this world. Those who are good at individual things and those who are good at organization. There are more of the former than of the latter. However, everyone has his strong points. He should be encouraged to develop and put to good use those strong points, however limited they may be. Even the lame, the dumb, the deaf, and the blind could all help in the revolutionary struggle." When Mao said this, he was a man of twenty-four, but they are words of remarkable maturity. They have a broadness of vision, a wideranging tolerance, not common anywhere, least of all among the Chinese student body of 1917.

Mao's days as a student in the First Normal School were now coming to an end, but there was one more organization in which he participated. As part of the response to the Western penetration of China, a great many Chinese had gone to Europe to study its institutions. In 1912 some returned students had founded a society to enable Chinese students to study in France and Germany, living simply and working while they were there. Mao, although less enthusiastic about the West than many of his contemporaries, was active in organizing the society in Hunan, and although he did not go abroad himself, the society was to provide him with a valuable link with other intellectual circles in China in the next year or so.

With all his activities Mao did not neglect his studies. When he had entered the First Normal School, he had been a competent essayist, but during his time there, and under the influence of a master known as Yuan Big Beard, he became exceptionally polished in his style. Perhaps the most important literary work he did in Changsha was an essay he wrote for *New Youth*. The article was a somewhat strained appeal to the youth of China to strengthen its body, rather as Mao himself had done with the Three Heroes, in order to support China better. What is of more importance is the emphasis Mao placed on the power of the will to overcome all difficulties. It is as if, even at this early stage in his career, Mao had a premonition of his future, when his survival and that of his party would depend on the unbroken will to survive.

In 1918 Mao finished his education in Hunan, and, having honorably passed his examinations, was awarded his diploma. He had entered the First Normal School six years previously a rough peasant lad, independently minded, curious, ready to fight for his beliefs, and with a knack for making friends. There is nothing unusual in any of these qualities—any building site or factory will have a dozen men who possess them—but Mao had other qualities: the power of organization, the ability to isolate essential detail, the knack of drawing other people into action. It was these that the social relationships of the college enabled to flower.

Underlying these qualities was the one gift without which all the others were merely attributes of the bureaucrat—imagination. Increasingly Mao was showing his capacity to think beyond the present. Many of his fellows were doing what he did; the New People's Study Society and the Association for Student Self-Government were not Mao's idea alone, and others were as active in them as he was. But there is no doubt that he brought a new dimension to them, relating them in a way to the real life of China. In addition, he was in earnest in what he was doing. Even in those days he gave the impression of a man who is not playing, not merely seeking the agreeable glories of a student leader.

To these qualities, the First Normal School had added extra dimensions. There he had been given an excellent education by tutors of high caliber, men who were original, traveled, and independent. Well aware of the need for change, they were equally conscious of the good aspects of

Chinese life and history, so that Mao was not subjected either to a denigration of his own country or to a contemptuous dismissal of the genuinely fruitful qualities of Western life.

And now Mao had to face the future. His normal course would have been to take a job, but, to the fury of his father, Mao made no attempt to begin earning his living. Instead he turned his face to the north and, with little more than the fare in his pocket, went to the capital of all China, the ancient city of Peking.

SEVEN

Mao was able to go to Peking as a result of his work in the Study Abroad movement. In response to an invitation from his teacher, Yang Ch'ang-chi, who had now taken a post at the National University in the capital, Mao, with other students from Changsha, went there to make final preparations for the departure of a large number of students who, it was hoped, would be allowed to go to France when World War I was over.

The men from Hunan, seven in all, rented a tiny room in Three Eyes Well Street, just behind the university. From this tiny base they handled the multitudinous details for the students' trip. Of course, they were not alone in this. Many eminent Chinese, eager to see Western ideas brought to China, were ready to help.

As the autumn faded and the winter drew in, the seven friends began to feel the pinch of hardship. Those among them who did have money had only a little, and most of them had none, Mao included. Their pooled resources stretched to a small meal each day and little else. The room they lived in had a "kang" or big Mongolian stove, but they could not afford wood for it. At night they slept on the stove, huddled together to keep warm. Years later, after experiences that made his winter in Peking seem like a picnic, Mao laughed at the memory. "If one of us wanted to turn over, we had to wake the others in case the one at the edge fell off," but it could have been no joke at the time.

Among themselves the friends had one overcoat, and when the weather was particularly cold, when the savage Manchruian winds swept across the city, they took turns wearing it. By January they had managed to get two more coats, but Mao never succeeded in getting one for himself. Even coatless in the bleak Peking winter, Mao was entranced by the beauty of the city and found it a "vivid compensation" for his hardship. He remembered especially the willows by the North Lake in the Forbidden City of the Emperors, their wands glittering with ice crystals, and, as the early northern spring quickened new life to growth, the white plum blossoms on Peking's million trees, flowering while the lakes were still locked in frozen silence.

With the coming of spring, the arrangements for the Study Abroad movement were completed and the first students made ready to go to France. All the men from Hunan were going except Mao.

On the face of it, it seems astonishing that Mao, after working so hard to organize the study program, should have turned down the chance to go abroad, and various reasons have been given for his decision. It has been said that he could not raise even the relatively small sum of money required and that he could not manage to learn enough French to make his way in France. Mao himself said that he did not go because he thought that he did not know enough about his own country.

All these reasons may be true, but there are two others worth considering. The lives of all men and women are made up of two influences: one is the relationship of a person to himself—his appetites, desires, talents, and fears; the other is the way he relates these feelings to the world outside himself, which, in turn, has its effect on him.

Perhaps these subtle, delicate, barely understood influences made Mao stay in China. The first, the desire, is easily stated. In Peking Mao had come to know Yang's daughter, Yang K'ai-hui, and at twenty-four, the earnest and puritanical young man had fallen in love. There could have been little possibility then that the love could come to anything. Even the liberal Yang was not likely to encourage a marriage between his daughter and a penniless student without a job.

However, despite being in love, Mao might well have gone to France except for his relationship to his country, which overrode all other considerations. This had never been simple; Mao was deeply critical of some aspects of his homeland, and an ardent admirer of others, but there is a sense in which, like Antaeus drawing his strength from the earth, Mao drew his strength from China. There he was at home in the profoundest sense, aware, perhaps in ways he himself scarcely understood, of the endless multiplicity of feelings, running as deeply as the deepest river, that go into making the emotional life of his nation. Indeed, if by saying that he did not know enough of his own country Mao meant that he still had to plumb those secret depths, then he may well have been speaking a truth more profound than even he knew then.

Mao stayed in Peking and faced a problem familiar to him: how to earn his living. Now the contacts he had made through the Study Abroad movement proved useful. The helpful Yang got in touch with the librarian of the university, Li Ta-chao, who gave Mao a job as library assistant. Mao hoped that through working at the university he would meet the leading intellectuals of China, but they, for the most part sheathed in the armor of social disdain which disfigured much of Chinese life, had no time for an obscure library assistant, who, moreover, spoke with a strong Hunanese accent.

By virtue of his position in the library, however, Mao was able to attend lectures, although so humble and therefore disagreeable was his position that lecturers refused to answer his questions. But one lecturer at least was approachable. This was the librarian, Li Ta-chao. He had founded a society in which Mao was welcomed and which was to have a crucial effect on Mao's life—a society for the study of Marxism.

Karl Marx, a German revolutionary, had developed certain theories about the nature of revolution and the role of different social classes in it. His experience was entirely European. He had never traveled outside Europe, and his theories were drawn from the life of that continent. To understand why the works of this man should be the focus of attention of a group of students in Peking, twelve thousand miles away from the scene of Marx's life, we must consider once more that enemy of capitalism which the West had unknowingly nurtured within itself—socialism.

The development of the socialist movement had taken two

directions. One had led to the formation of powerful social-democratic parties which, although they proposed the destruction of capitalism, thought that this could and should be done by democratic means—by the capture of the control of the State through the ballot box. The other direction had led to revolutionary parties which held that in no circumstances would capitalism allow itself to be transformed and that the only way to establish socialism was through the forcible overthrow of the ruling class. This would be done, the revolutionaries believed, by the revolt of the industrial working class—a class which was doomed to be exploited forever by the capitalists, but which, through its experience in communal labor, would be able to unite its power and, because of its increasingly miserable conditions, in the last resort would not shrink from using that power.

Karl Marx had hammered out this theory, and Marxism, as it was called, had gained its adherents in Europe, although its most serious followers were in countries such as Russia, where freedom of speech and organization were denied. Ironically for a theory that placed so much stress on the leading role of the industiral working class, these countries were the least industrialized in Europe.

Up to 1917 Marxism had, in practical terms, meant little. It was the social-democratic organizations of Europe, such as the British Labour Party, that were growing in strength and influence. As a serious belief, revolutionary Marxism was the concern mainly of small groups of refugees from the despotism of Russia. But the war, which was crippling the West, bled Russia to death. Appalling losses in battle, starvation at home, an incompetent government led by an autocratic and ineffectual tsar led to a spontaneous uprising of its largely peasant population and the overthrow of the monarchy.

The tsar's government was replaced by one which had pretensions to democracy but which, in an act of staggering ineptitude, announced that it was to carry on with the war. Since the Revolution had taken place because the tsar had followed that very policy, it is not surprising that this government in its turn was overthrown. In the confusion that followed, power was seized by the only party that promised to stop the war—the revolutionary Marxist party known as the Bolshevik Party, led by Lenin. This seizure of power was hailed as a victory for Marx's theory, despite the fact that there was not a very significant number of industrial workers in Russia and that the leadership of the Bolsheviks was entirely middle-class.

Until the Revolution the Chinese had not been particularly interested in Russia. Russia had attacked China in the nineteenth century, but as defeat by the Japanese had shown, Russia was hardly less decrepit than China itself and had little to offer China either in ideas or technology. However, the Revolution attracted interest among some thoughtful Chinese. After all, Russia, like China, had been an autocratic regime, and its resources had also come from a vast rural community. If indeed the Revolution was to lead Russia to a new, vigorous, and modern life, then it and the theory that underlay it were worthy of study.

Among the group of earnest Chinese who began their study of Marxism under the flickering oil lamps of the university library in Peking in the spring of 1918, none understood or even accepted Marx's ideas. The elegant Li was an advocate of parliamentary democracy, and Mao was more interested in anarchism—an even more extreme revolutionary theory. But even while studying the theories of Marx, Mao did not lose his grip on his own background. He made serious efforts to combine Marxism with the philosophy of ancient China. His commitment to Marxism and communism would have to wait until history imposed its own unexpected logic on him. His commitment to China was with him always.

More students were now ready to go to France, and this time Mao went south with them, both to say good-bye and to take the opportunity to see more of China, especially Shanghai. The major port of China, and of all its cities the one most under the domination of foreigners, Shanghai was where the Western control of China's economy was most obvious.

Mao began his journey to Shanghai more in hope than expectancy, for, penniless as ever, he could afford a ticket only to Tientsin, a hundred miles from Peking, which left him with another seven hundred miles to go. At Tientsin station, however, he met one of his ubiquitous friends, who lent him money for a ticket to Nanking. On his way Mao stopped off at Chu-fu, the burial place of Confucius. There, too, he made a pilgrimage to other historic sites, all of them representative of a history an ardent modernist might be expected to find repugnant but which had for Mao the aura of China's unique and invincible past.

Once again Mao had run out of money, and in his curiously absentminded way he lost his shoes. However, he seems to have had a horde of friends wandering across China, for he met another who lent him enough money for the rest of his journey and for a new pair of shoes. It is worth noting Mao's friendships. People who knew Mao at this time often commented on his reserved manner, but he had an extraordinarily wide range of friends, all of whom were ready to lend him money, although they must have known that not only had he had none for the previous five years, but that there was little obvious chance of his having any in the future. People make friends—and especially friends who will lend them money—only if they have a special quality about them that evokes trust. Mao obviously had this, and in the years to come his future was to depend on just this ability to make people trust him.

Finally Mao reached Shanghai. His stay there was not long, although later he and many of the men and women he saw off on their journey were to have the name of the gray city burned in their hearts. But brief though his stay may have been, there was one sight he would certainly have seen: the infamous sign in the park reserved for foreigners, which read, "Dogs and Chinese not allowed."

With that message in the back of his mind, Mao took a train back to Changsha and whatever the future might bring him.

EIGHT

Mao took a room outside Changsha, across the Hsiang, and from his window he looked across the river to a troubled city. The governor of Hunan, Chang Ching-yao, was another in the dismal procession of brutal soldiers the National Revolution had brought to power. His disgustingly rapacious behavior was causing deep unrest, especially among the students, and their hatred of him was deepened because he was an ally of General Tuan Ch'i-jui, who was the real master of the corrupt so-called National Government in Peking. This was of concern to the students—and not only them—because Tuan was pro-Japanese.

No patriot felt anything but fear and dislike of Japan, although there was a kind of reluctant admiration for its power. Japan's industrial might was a sword poised over China, and warlords, ruthless and efficient, were ready to use that sword. Korea, Taiwan, and South Manchuria had already been wrenched away from China by Japan; the Twenty-One Demands had actually been an attempt to control China proper, and Japan's continuing interference in Chinese affairs kept Chinese resentment simmering. Tuan Ch'i-jui was a conductor for this resentment because he was supported by Japanese money, in exchange for his goodwill.

In 1919 Chinese resentment boiled over. As Mao established himself in Changsha, on the other side of the world,

45

in the Palace of Versailles, the victorious Allied powers were
meeting to discuss the terms they were to exact from Germany. Among the victors were both Japan and China, who
had entered the war in 1917. But in the eyes of the great
powers—France, Britain, and the United States—the two
Eastern allies presented different pictures: China, ragged,
ramshackle, an object of derision; and Japan, united, efficient,
armed to the teeth, and, if it wished to be, a threat to the
West's all-important trade routes to the East.

Well aware of its importance, Japan was about to present
its bill for its part in the war. Its foremost demand was that
the former German territories in China should now be
Japan's—and an appalled China discovered that the West was
ready to hand over the spoils.

The news created an outburst of popular feeling that shook
all China. On May 4, in Peking, thousands of students
marched in an enormous procession, demanded that the government refuse the terms, and burned down the house of the
most pro-Japanese minister. General Tuan moved his troops
against the demonstrators, but they would not be stopped.
The jails of Peking were crammed with students, but still the
demonstrators marched. The trouble not only continued but
spread. In the great ports dockers refused to handle Japanese
goods; merchants would not deal in them. The China of the
cities was united for the first time in living memory, and not
all the clubs and bayonets of the generals could break that
unity.

Changsha, too, was united, and in June, to give edge to the
protest, a United Students' Association was formed. Mao, still
in the New People's Study Society, took a leading part in organizing the United Students' Association and in founding a
new magazine, the *Hsiang River Review*.

The magazine was edited, produced, and written largely by
Mao, and it was extremely important to him. Up till now
Mao had been known to relatively few people: the students
at the First Normal School, his fellow infantrymen in the
army, the small and isolated group in Peking. Now his voice
was heard across the province, and farther than that. In July
he wrote an article urging a "Union of the Great Popular
Masses," not only to defeat the Japanese demands, but to
lead China from its morass. In this article he hailed the Russian Revolution as the vanguard of the liberators of the

oppressed nations, and described the poor people of the world as the "Army of the Red Flag."

Mao's incisive voice, cutting through the stratification of Chinese society and calling for an end to despair, was heard and noted by the intellectuals of Peking, and it was also heard by the semi-literate shopkeepers and workers along the Hsiang River. Anyone with the merest smattering of Chinese could understand Mao because he wrote in a deliberately simplified form of the language first designed by Ch'en Tu-hsiu.

The *Hsiang River Review* did not have a long life. Chang Ching-yao closed the magazine down. It may well have been the use of the simplified language, rather than what was said, that prompted his action. Any voice of dissent was unpopular with the Changsha authorities: one that was understood by the great mass of people was doubly so. But having lost the *Hsiang River Review*, Mao turned to another student magazine and carried on with his determined opposition to the pro-Japanese generals running China. And when, in turn, Chang closed down this magazine. Mao started writing articles for the daily newspaper. In these he continued to attack Chang Ching-yao and to support the May Fourth Movement, but he was dealing with broader issues as well.

Of particular interest are those articles he wrote concerning women. It is typical of modern revolution that the role of women has been debated. Revolutions are, at least in name, about human rights, and women have long been the class most obviously deprived of them. This was particularly so in China, where women were without legal rights of any kind. The majority of them were treated as mere beasts of burden and frequently regarded as being less valuable than animals. Mao, as an ardent idealist, would naturally have the cause of women at heart; in the China of 1919 it would have taken a stony or an ignorant heart not to be moved by their plight. But possibly there were other reasons for Mao's passionate and repeated articles about women that summer. His close relationship with Yang K'ai-hui must have made him feel personally involved with women's rights. Mao's mother had recently died, and it is difficult not to think of his being moved by this. Twenty years after her death Mao spoke with deep affection of the gentle, devout, and obedient woman who typified all the oppressed and despised womankind of China.

Chang was growing increasingly restless at the opposition to him. At first, faced with the massive resistance of the city, he had moved carefully, even nervously, in dealing with the agitation, but now, as winter moved in, he was beginning to show his hand. In December Mao called a students' strike aimed directly at the overthrow of Chang. The infuriated governor called the student leaders to his palace and warned them to stop meddling with political matters, threatening to have their heads cut off if they continued. The threat may not have been altogether serious, although the executioner and his ax was a common sight on the streets of Chinese cities, but it frightened the students. Mao, however, was contemptuous and said that Chang was no more than a barking dog. Even Mao's enemies never questioned his fearlessness, but his attitude toward Chang was more than mere hardihood; it has a moral quality about it, the sort of bravery people who belong to a good cause have when faced with brutes.

Brave though Mao was, he did not want martyrdom, and conditions in Changsha were becoming extremely dangerous. As it was now clear that Chang would not be overthrown by action from within Hunan, the Students' Associations chose delegates to find arms stronger than theirs which might strike Chang from his seat of power.

Mao was chosen to go to Peking, and not by accident. In the seven months that he had been in Changsha, his position had altered beyond recognition. He was no longer an obscure provincial student, but a man known to the leading thinkers. His articles in the *Hsiang River Review* had been widely read, and reviewed in the most important journals. But Mao may have wanted to go to Peking, anyway, for although his old friend and tutor, Yang, had died, Yang's daughter K'ai-hui was still there.

Whatever pleasure Mao got from seeing K'ai-hui again, he got little joy from his attempt to gain help against Chang. The fearsome warlords of Peking were hardly likely to move against their own man, and without help from other soldiers the people of Hunan could not hope to remove their governor. Disappointed, Mao left Peking for Shanghai, but not before he had read a book which, except for the Bible, has altered the lives of more people than any other book ever written—the *Communist Manifesto*.

The *Manifesto* was the fighting document that proclaimed, in simple vigorous prose, the basic beliefs of Marx and Engels, the founders of the communist movement. Despite Mao's previous studies of Marxism, it was from the reading of this book that his real commitment to communism dated, and it is worth hazarding a guess that it was the vigorous, battling tone of the *Manifesto* that captured Mao's equally martial imagination.

With a copy of the *Manifesto* in his pocket, Mao arrived in Shanghai. This time he had not needed to borrow for his journey, but even as a figure of some note, he was still virtually penniless. Penniless but not at all proud, for in Shanghai he took a job as a laundryman.

Although Shanghai was the city in China most dominated by foreigners and had become a symbol of oppression, it was, nevertheless, a refuge for many Chinese who were being hounded by the Peking government. Its many foreign concessions held useful hiding places. In one of them Mao found Ch'en Tu-hsiu, the Dean of Letters of Peking University, who was resting after being imprisoned for his part in the May Fourth Movement. In jail, he, too, had become deeply interested in Marxism. Mao, no longer the despised library assistant, became involved with him in lengthy discussions on the nature of the theory and its application to Chinese affairs. It is indicative of the rate of change in China that the august Ch'en could have such conversations with a laundryman—even a temporary laundryman.

Mao once said that at this period of his life these talks with Ch'en were of extreme importance. Ch'en's status as a thinker was high, his work in editing *New Youth* had been of enormous importance in Mao's development, and his patriotism was undoubted. That such a man should have been seriously considering communism must have had a powerful effect on Mao.

But in Shanghai Mao met another man who was to have a more immediate effect on his future. This was an old teacher of his from the First Normal School, called I Pei-chi.

I Pei-chi had been a strong supporter of the Alliance Party, more properly called the Kuomintang, from its earliest days. Forced to leave Changsha by Chang Ching-yao, he was now in Pengyang, outside Shanghai, plotting the overthrow of Chang. I Pei-chi was in close contact with T'an Yen-k'ai, who had been governor of Changsha in the National Revolution of 1911 and who had great influence among the officers of the New Model Army. Strong forces of the army stationed on the Kwangtung-Hunan border, where the Kuomintang influence was strongest, were ready to follow T'an if he decided to attack Chang. It was the plans for such an attack that the two men were preparing when Mao appeared.

Mao was a useful ally for I and T'an; he had excellent contacts among the revolutionary students inside the city. He was invited to join the plotters. Throughout the spring of 1920 the three men prepared their plans, and in June they were ready to strike. The Kwangtung army marched into Hunan without opposition, and Chang fled. I Pei-chi, as a friend of the new governor, T'an, was extremely influential and had a number of important posts at his disposal. One of these was that of head of the junior section of the First Normal School, and he gave this post to Mao.

This transformation of Mao's fortunes seems, at first, astonishing. Only a year previously he had been filing newspapers in the dim recesses of Peking University, hardly more important than a janitor. Now he walked the streets of Changsha an important man in his own right, possessing the prestige of his post, the friendship of the governor, and for the first time in his life a substantial income of his own.

However, the change was not so magical as it might seem. Ability finds its own level, and there is no doubt that Mao was an able man. More important, in a time of violent change he was allied to a group which, although at this time struggling for its existence, was nevertheless a mighty and growing force and the heir to China's future. It is worth remembering that Mao was not allied to the Kuomintang out of personal ambition. If this had been the case he would no doubt have remained in it when it ruled all China. He supported the Kuomintang because, like many others, he saw in it the best hope for China, just as when, later on, he gave up power and office and became a hunted fugitive in the Chinese Communist Party, he saw in that desperate adventure the best way to serve his nation.

But that was for the future. Now, in 1920, Mao's own future seemed secure. The Kuomintang was growing in strength, and as it rose to power, so he might well have risen with it. But already his country was feeling the first faint tremors of the revolutionary earthquake in Russia, and this was soon to send out greater shock waves that were to alter the course of China's future and change the lives of every being in it.

It had taken three years for the Russian Revolution to affect China directly. For the first two years of the Revolution, as its leaders struggled to gain control of European Russia, the vastness of Siberia was in the hands of various anti-communist groups. However, as the revolutionaries tightened their grip on western Russia, they were able to turn to their eastern possessions, and by 1920, after a series of running battles along the trans-Siberian railway, they had mastered their enemies and were rulers of the old tsarist empire, from the borders of Poland to the Aleutian Islands.

The southern borders of the new republic ran along Turkey, Iran, Afghanistan, Tibet, and China, and this physical contiguity brought with it political problems. What were the relationships of Russia with its neighbors to be? Whatever their attitude in years to come, at this time the Russian leaders were idealistic. Having renounced inequality at home, they were ready to renounce it abroad. They believed that the treaties that the tsarist government had made with its weak neighbors were unjust, and they were ready to renegotiate them. Of all these old treaties the one with China was manifestly the most unjust, and in 1920 the revolutionary government renounced all their claims to Chinese territory.

The effect of this on the Chinese was immense. At a time when the Versailles Treaty was still fresh and bitter in Chinese minds, they saw a great power, for the first time since the eighteenth century, behaving with tact and generosity toward them.

Russia's action gave an added stimulus to those Chinese who were studying Marxism. Now they became increasingly interested in the Russian system of communism. In turn, the Russians became increasingly interested in China. Obviously it was in China's interest to have a friendly neighbor at her back door, and if that neighbor was communist too, so much the better.

In 1920 a communist organization known as the Third International sent a delegate, Gregor Voitinsky, to China to contact friendly Chinese. In Peking Voitinsky met Li Ta-chao, whose Marxist study group Mao had attended, and Li gave him the address of Ch'en Tu-hsiu. Voitinsky met Ch'en in Shanghai and, following conversations together, Ch'en founded a Marxist group in the city.

Mao, in close touch with Ch'en, was well aware of these developments and founded a Marxist group in Changsha. For the members of this group, he recruited from the New People's Study Society, which was still going strong, and also from various labor organizations that Mao had been helping to organize. But politics were not the whole of Mao's life at this time. For the past year he had been courting Yang K'ai-hui, and in the winter of 1920 they married. Yang K'ai-hui was a small, pale girl, serious-minded, and, like her father, an excellent scholar. That she and Mao should have married at all is evidence of how far Mao had progressed during the past year or so. Before his unexpected promotion there could have been no question of his marrying the daughter of a man like Yang. But just as China's increasingly revolutionary politics had brought Mao and K'ai-hui together, so in a few years' time it was to part them and in so tragic a manner that it was to haunt Mao for the rest of his life.

Throughout the winter following his marriage Mao was incredibly active in Changsha. As well as running his school and founding his Marxist group, he was working with the labor organizations, writing for the newspapers, and running a radical bookshop. There is an amusing anecdote about the shop that also illustrates Mao's coolness, which could verge on impudence. The governor, T'an, was proud of his handwriting, and Mao talked him into painting the sign for the shop—although whether T'an really knew the nature of the books being sold there is problematical.

While Mao organized his Marxists in Changsha, other men in other cities, equally attracted by communist theory, were also organizing groups. And not only in China. In France and Germany Chinese students were coming together as Marxists. From Shanghai Voitinsky watched the groups develop. He had now been joined by another agent of the Russians, a Dutchman, Hendricus Sneevliet, who had come from the Dutch East Indies, where he had been organizing communist groups. In July 1921 the two men called a meeting of all the Marxist groups of China, for they had decided the time was ripe to form a Communist Party of China.

NINE

The Chinese have many proverbs, but when one thinks about the founding of the Chinese Communist Party, none is more appropriate than the one that says, "A journey of a thousand miles starts with a single step." For in that July, among the hundreds of millions who lived in China's immensity, only seventy or eighty people were, or even thought they were, Marxists, and of that handful only twelve were called to the first meeting of the party.

They met in Shanghai in the steamy heat of summer, filtering in from Canton and Peking and Changsha, and the meeting was no holiday jaunt. To be a revolutionary in the China of the warlords was to put one's head close to the ax. Because of this the meeting was held in the French Concession, where the Chinese police had no authority, and, incongruously, in a girls' school that had closed for the summer vacation. The French police, however, were no more welcoming than their Chinese counterparts—and a good deal more efficient. Within a day they were shadowing the delegates, whereupon the delegates decided to leave Shanghai.

Their next meeting took place on a lake near Chiahsing, a popular resort near Shanghai. The Marxists hired a boat, and, in the guise of jocular pleasure-seekers, they sailed about the tranquil waters of the lake in a steady rain and hammered out their program.

The crucial point in their declaration was that the Chinese Communist Party would aim at winning over the industrial working class, the "proletariat," and that they would do this alone, without collaborating with any other group or party. This was a faithful enough echo of Marx's teaching, but it is astonishing that intelligent men should have seen it as a priority in China, for it bore no relationship to the realities of Chinese life. There was no industrial working class, or, rather, none of importance. The great cities had factories, the ports had docks, inland there were railways and mines, but the numbers who worked in them were infinitesimal compared to the great mass of those who worked on the land.

The point caused fierce disagreement among the Chinese Communists, both then and for years to come, but for the present the decision stood, and as they parted in the rain, the delegates were confident that they had laid the foundation for a new and formidable political force in China.

The first task of the Communist Party was to build up its membership, and in Changsha Mao began this task with his customary drive and determination. He was aided by his wife, who now was also a Communist, and by Li Li-san, the man who had been the silent listener who had answered Mao's "Twenty-Eight-Stroke-Character" advertisement in 1917. Ardent comrades now, Li and Mao were to become locked in bitter enmity in the years to come.

In the winter of 1922 the Communists were working hard at their new task. From the Marxist study group he had organized the previous spring, Mao recruited members of the Communist Party, and in the Ch'uan-shan Hsue-she, where he had studied the works of Wang Fu-chih, Mao started a Self-Study University, where students could study independently, as he himself had done before entering the First Normal School. Of course, many of the books made available were Marxist, as were the lecturers who volunteered their time, but, true to Mao's own instincts, the students were also encouraged to study the traditional writers, thus maintaining that deep taproot that drew nourishment from China's past.

Mao was also quite ready to use other organizations. The Chinese branch of the Young Men's Christian Association, financed by American money, had already started a "mass education" movement in a genuine effort to spread literacy among the poor. It had special textbooks written in the simplified characters, but Mao unscrupulously used the program to have special books written that taught Marxism.

As Mao drove through his schemes, it was beginning to look as if the Chinese Communists' belief in the power of the working class were well founded, after all. Although the peasantry was helpless before its oppressors, the industrial workers, as Marx had noted, had the weapon of the strike. In the winter of 1920 and 1921 the workers had used this weapon to some effect. Wages were raised and working conditions improved. Mao was active in organizing the strikes, but he was not alone. Many other left-wing politicians—socialists, who believe in moderate government, and anarchists, who believed in no government—joined with the Communist Party members. Hunan now had a new governor. T'an had left to work with the Kuomintang and had been replaced by a less restrained man, Colonel Chao, who had commanded Mao's regiment in 1911. Chao had no time for labor organizers, and to make his views clear, he had two anarchist leaders dragged into the street and shot.

This action led to the creation of a United Labor Front, and the coordinated activities of the left led to renewed struggles. Two great strikes among the miners and the railwaymen of the Canton-Hankow railway began to make it seem as if Marx's thesis about the power of the industrial worker were as true for China as for Europe. But if this seemed so to the Chinese, other, bleaker eyes had seen the weakness of the Chinese position, and, from afar, they called the Chinese to heel.

In January 1922 the Russians called a meeting, known as the Congress of the Toilers of the Far East. Both the Chinese Communists and the Kuomintang sent delegates—the Communists because Russia was their spiritual home, the Kuomintang for other reasons.

Sun Yat-sen had already been in contact with the Russians, who had offered to give him the financial aid the West had refused, advice on reorganizing the Kuomintang, and, most important, arms. It was an offer Sun could not refuse. Russian arms would free him from dependence on the fickle favors of the warlords and help him to reunite China. He accepted—and was ready to pay the price, which was the admission of Communists into the Kuomintang.

Sun having been persuaded, it was next the turn of the

Communists. They were not enamored of the proposed alliance. After all, they considered themselves the chosen party that would rule China, and the Russians were not offering *them* arms. But at the Congress of the Toilers of the Far East the Russians made it clear why they should accept the new situation. The Chinese were told that, though Marx did indeed believe that the Communist Party was the only party capable of leading the revolution, he had also taught that before this could happen history had to go through various stages. Before there could be a workers' revolution there must first be a bourgeois revolution—that is, the middle classes had to gain power from the landowning class. As this bourgeois revolution had not yet taken place in China, the Communists would have to wait their turn, or rather, assist the middle class—the Kuomintang—to have its revolution so that the real revolution would come sooner.

The Russians placed enormous stress on this policy. They saw themselves as the standard-bearers of communism for the whole world, a world dominated by capitalist powers which were aiming at the overthrow of the Russian state. Their aim was to break the power of capitalism on a global scale, and Lenin had said that this power would be smashed only when the West had lost the source of its strength, the colonial empires. In a famous phrase he had declared that capitalism would be broken on the banks of the Nile, the Ganges, and the Yangtze. Now, Lenin declared, was the time of the Yangtze, and the Chinese Communists must help by supporting the anti-Western Kuomintang.

This was what the Russians wanted; it was what Sun Yat-sen had agreed to. Now all that was required was for the Chinese Communist Party to assent. In July 1922, at its Second Congress, the C.C.P. duly agreed. In this enormously important decision one voice was missing—that of Mao Tse-tung. He was actually in Shanghai when the party met, but missed it because, he said, he forgot the address and, although he roamed around Shanghai looking for the meeting, failed to find it.

This at any rate was Mao's story, and it may well be true. We have seen before this his oddly impractical manner and dreamy ways, but to forget where an event as important as the Second Congress of his party was meeting is truly extraordinary. It is tempting to speculate whether Mao didn't forget on purpose, as it were, in order not to have any part in the decision to collaborate with the Kuomintang.

If this was a motive, and it is merely a suggestion, then events were to change Mao's mind. The previous year the labor organizations in Changsha had been strong enough to march through its streets under the Red banner, but in 1923 Wu P'ei-fu, the pro-English warlord of the Yangtze Basin, whom the Communists had supported against his rivals in exchange for the freedom to organize the workers, turned his guns on the strikers on the Wuhan railway and slaughtered them. The lesson was too obvious to miss. After all, the workers were too isolated, too small in numbers, too defenseless to lead the revolution. And so, with the smoke of Wu P'ei-fu's guns to remind them of the realities of Chinese life, the Chinese Communists threw themselves into cooperation with the party of Sun Yat-sen.

Not all the Communists were keen on this policy. Ch'en, for instance, still longed for a totally independent party, but others were wholehearted in their support, and none more so than Mao. In 1919 he had called for a "Great Union of the Popular Masses"; now, under the white banners of the Kuomintang, it was possible to see that union being forged. It was also being armed, for, true to its promise, the Soviet Union had sent military advisers and weapons, and on the banks of the Whampoa River at Canton a military academy had been opened under a brilliant young soldier, Colonel Chiang Kai-shek.

In this new, broad movement Mao began to take a leading part. His own party nominated him as a delegate to the Executive Committee of the Kuomintang, and so enthusiastically did he work that he came under suspicion from the Chinese Communist Party as lacking in loyalty. This suspicion showed the difficulty facing both parties. Sun had no intention of allowing the Kuomintang to become the tool of the fanatically dedicated Communists, and they were always aware of the danger they faced in strengthening the Kuomintang. If it became too strong, then, like Frankenstein's monster, it might be able to dispense with its master.

Mao was either unaware of these dangers or ignored them, for he worked so hard for the Kuomintang that in the winter of 1924 even his sturdy frame felt the strain and he fell ill. To recuperate he returned to his home in Shaoshan village.

It was the first time Mao had returned home since, a hopeful young student, he had left for Tungshan fifteen years previously, and it was his first prolonged stay in the countryside since he had begged his way across Hunan with Siao Yu in 1912. What Mao was now to see was to alter his whole way of thinking about China.

In 1912 Mao had seen a relatively tranquil countryside. Law and custom were still strong, and a semblance of order was maintained. But since then had come the rule of the warlords. For them, the peasants, endlessly at their patient toil, were no more than cattle to be milked and, if necessary, slaughtered. The armies of the warlords battened on the land, looting, pillaging, butchering. To escape this anarchy the merchants had withdrawn to the cities, and with them went the landlords. They left behind them only their rent collectors, who took much and gave little. The mandarins went too, and with them the vestiges of the old Confucian order. Now the Chinese countryside staggered to disaster. Great dikes and canals, the very arteries of China, built and maintained over not hundreds but thousands of years, crumbled and decayed. Flood drowned the peasants' toil, drought withered it, and famine rattled its dry bones before every door.

But as the economy of the countryside had changed, so had the peasantry. They were fighting back, and not only fighting: they were banding together to take the land for themselves. Hunan, Mao found, was riddled with village organizations that had confiscated land and were sharing it on something very close to collective principles. In fact, while the Communist Party had been debating the revolutionary potential of the industrial workers, the revolution itself had already come to the countryside.

Mao was stirred by what he saw. And from now on he was to see with increasing clarity and force that the key to the revolution lay with the peasants. In this Mao was closer to the Kuomintang than to his own party. The Kuomintang, looking of course for a different kind of revolution, had already seen that the peasants were a crucial factor in China's rebirth and had set up a Peasant Training Institute to develop organizers who could give point and purpose to the peasant revolt. Mao himself was to become the head of the Peasant Training Institute, but not before an event of enormous importance had occurred.

In May 1925 the Communists active in Shanghai organized strikes in textile mills owned by the Japanese. One of the strikers was killed by a Japanese foreman, and this led to massive demonstrations. On May 30, a demonstration took place outside the British Concession, and the police, under the orders of an Englishman, fired and killed ten people. A few days later there were more shootings and more deaths. The result was an explosion of savage hatred and resentment. In other strike violence, at least the offenders had been Chinese, but now Chinese were being shot down on China's sacred soil by the hated and despised foreigners.

Once again China became united. Shanghai came to a halt as workers closed down the factories and docks, merchants the shops, and bankers the banks. The disturbances spread down the coast. In Canton the French and British again used their guns, this time killing more than fifty people. The sense of outrage the Chinese felt was not confined to the cities; it spread into the countryside in a way that had not happened in China for many years. And the shootings raised a question: the hated foreigners had done the shooting, but who had allowed them to do it? The answer to that was the warlords, the military men who ruled China for twelve years. Peasants, workers, students, landlords, mandarins—all could see that. And further, all could see that the Kuomintang opposed the warlords. Where there is unity of understanding, there is unity of purpose, and in 1925 the unity of China had begun to cohere around the Kuomintang and Sun Yat-sen.

Already the Kuomintang was showing its new teeth. Its army, Soviet trained, Soviet armed, but commanded by Chiang Kai-shek, struck at the warlord of Kwangtung, Chien Ch'ung-ming, and destroyed him. Now, as the country swung behind him, Sun Yat-sen ordered Chiang to prepare for the next blow—a great expedition to the north, where the Kuomintang would end the pro-Japanese government and destroy the rule of the warlord.

As the Communists and Nationalists fought their battles in Canton and Shanghai and as Chiang Kai-shek, who was now the general commanding all the Kuomintang armies, prepared his forces for the great Northern Expedition, Mao was still in Hunan. But once more his activities attracted the attention of the governor, Chao Heng-t'i, and he had to flee to Canton. Both Sun Yat-sen and Chiang were as aware as

Mao of the importance of the peasantry—especially of the help it could give the army as it marched north—and it was with their approval that Mao was made head of a peasant department.

Already the unity of the Communist Party and the Kuomintang was beginning to crack. Many of the officers in the Kuomintang army were from landowning families, and although they were patriotic, they had no wish to see any revolutionary changes in the ownership of the land. These officers were increasingly suspicious of the Communists. When the Kuomintang army had marched into Kwangtung the previous year, they had seen Communists organizing the peasants and confiscating land. In the districts known as Halu-feng the Communists had actually formed a state within a state, changing the tax system and expropriating the land, although without the approval of the Central Committee—the ruling body of the Chinese Communist Party.

The businessmen in the cities were also uneasy at the prospects of Communists in the government, for just as the Communists were ready to confiscate land, so were they ready to take over businesses. So, inside the Kuomintang as the summer of 1925 wore away, a group that could be termed the right wing was developing in opposition to the Communists and their allies, who might be called left wing.

The Communists too were restive. They were the weakest group inside the Kuomintang and they were frightened that the right wing, the armed body, might turn on them. A complicating factor for them also was that, following the death of Lenin in 1924, the Soviets had begun to alter their attitude toward the Kuomintang. The new leaders of the U.S.S.R., Stalin and Trotsky, were concerned for the security of the Chinese Eastern Railway, partly owned by them and a vital link to the U.S.S.R.'s Asian possessions, which Chang Tso-lin, the new master of the Peking government, threatened to nationalize. More concerned with their own security than with the success of the Kuomintang, the Soviets told Sun Yat-sen that they were going to recognize Chang Tso-lin as lawful ruler of North China and Sun as ruler of the South. Nothing could have shown more clearly Soviet ignorance of China. The unity of the nation was the prime concern of every Chinese patriot, and there was absolutely no possibility of the Kuomintang's accepting such a scheme. This was made clear to Stalin, and the implied threat was withdrawn. But this did little to help the Chinese Communists, who, closely identified with the Soviet Union, were regarded with more and more suspicion by the Kuomintang.

To make matters worse for them, Sun Yat-sen, the very symbol of the unity of the Kuomintang and a moderating influence in the rivalry between the left and the right, died in March 1925, and real power passed into the hands of Chiang Kai-shek, the dedicated soldier, who had no love whatever for Communism.

In these circumstances many of the Communists thought that the Chinese Communist Party should leave the Kuomintang altogether. Mao, however, who was not only head of the Peasant Training Institute but Director of the Propaganda Department, was in favor of keeping the alliance. Although the leadership of the Chinese Communists still clung to their Marxist dogmas and believed that the industrial working class of the cities would bring about the revolution, Mao was increasingly impressed by what he had seen of the peasants in Hunan the previous year. "Every party," he said, "needs a center of gravity. The center of gravity for the Kuomintang is hidden among the countless masses of the exploited peasantry." As the forthcoming Northern Expedition moved across the countryside, he foresaw that the peasants would be roused to a revolutionary fury that would change the social order of China, and that if the Communist Party was still working with the Kuomintang, then it would be in the best position to influence the shape of the new social order.

Accordingly, Mao threw his weight onto the side arguing for the maintenance of the alliance and, in fact, the threatened split did not take place, for, faced with Chiang's determination, the Russians dropped their suggestion for the division of China and rallied around Chiang Kai-shek's policy, at the same time ordering the Chinese Communists to stay inside the Kuomintang.

In this confused state of affairs, with the right wing of the Kuomintang more and more threatening, the Soviets dithering, and the Chinese Communists seriously split among themselves, Chiang led the armies of the Kuomintang across the Kwangtung border in the opening campaign of the great Northern Expedition.

TEN

Through the early summer of 1926 the armies of the Kuomintang marched north, across Kiangsi and Hunan. Before Chiang's troops, well armed, well led, patriotic, the ragged armies of the warlords were scattered like chaff. Behind the Kuomintang's armies, as Mao had prophesied, the peasants rose in a fury of vengeance. And among the peasants moved the men from the Peasant Training Institute, Mao's own brother Mao Tse-min among them. Left wing to a man, they organized the peasants into socialist groups, redistributing land, paying off scores against old masters, burning rent rolls.

But as the Northern Expedition made its triumphant progress, the division in its ranks was becoming more serious. The officer corps of the army was increasingly sullen as on their march north the fires they ignited burned *their* property and the land redistribution took from them their own land. In July the army swung northwest and established itself at Nanchang, while the government had moved into Wuhan, north of the army, on the Yangtze. This physical division of army and government symbolized the rift between them, for as the army was right wing, so the government was left wing or, at any rate, influenced by the Left.

Throughout the summer the government in Wuhan held debates on the major problem facing it, the cause of the dissension between its two wings—the problem of land reform.

Mao made his position clear: in Hunan, he said, the peasants had already reformed the land. All the government had to do was legalize their actions. The Communist Party, still hankering after the revolution of the cities, and meekly following Stalin's instructions that the Kuomintang victory must come before any other action, argued that land reform must take place slowly and only under the strictest limitations. The Kuomintang itself was increasingly vague about what it wanted, and its members, nominally left, were subdividing into groups that were more or less radical.

The right Kuomintang, the left Kuomintang, and the Communists argued the summer away, but the fate of this, the second National Revolution, did not lie in their hands. Power was in the grip of the generals, and none of them had a stronger fist than the heir to Sun Yat-sen, Chiang Kai-shek.

Chiang, who had been so fervent a believer in the role of the peasantry the year before, had, like his officers, grown colder toward the Communists. Now he sat with his troops about him in Nanchang, watching the government in Wuhan, and as he watched them, so he was being watched himself. From their warehouses and offices in the great cities, the merchants had seen the near revolution in the countryside and waited with increasing alarm for the social upheaval to reach them. As with the landlords, their fears were not groundless. Shanghai in particular had a massive labor movement led by dedicated Communists. In March 1927 officers of the Kuomintang army met Chinese businessmen in the Concessions of Shanghai, and with them were representatives from the Western powers. The foreigners made it clear that the changes in China alarmed them as much as they frightened the Chinese. If the Communist menace was neutralized, they said, then they would be ready to aid the Kuomintang and make certain concessions on the unequal treaties.

Chiang was informed of these talks, but what he made of them he kept to himself. For a week he kept his army leashed in Nanchang. The government in Wuhan ordered him to cross the Yangtze and march on Peking, but he ignored the order, nor did he, as some feared, turn on the government itself. Instead, he turned his army east, down the Yangtze to the western stronghold of Shanghai.

Inside the city the Communist Party made its plans to welcome Chiang. Led by a man called Chou En-lai, the Communists and the trade unions organized a series of strikes that paralyzed the city. An armed assault group seized the arsenal and the barracks. Within a few weeks the whole of the city was in the hands of the Communists, and the troops of the warlord had surrendered or fled.

On March 21 Chiang appeared outside the city and was welcomed by the Communist militia. On April 12, to the sound of a trumpet call, he unleashed his troops against them. In the next weeks five thousand Communists were butchered by the stammering machine guns of the Kuomintang and by the knives of the criminal gangs whom Chiang recruited for the slaughter.

Some escaped. Chou En-lai slipped from the grasp of the army, but the leadership of the Communist Party in the city was destroyed and Ch'en Tu-hsiu lost his son. As Chiang wiped out the Communists of Shanghai, Chang Tso-lin struck at the Communists of Peking. Nineteen leading Communists were murdered there, including the elegant and learned Li Ta-chao, who was strangled. In Canton, too, the massacre continued, but worse was to come. In May Chiang came out in open revolt against the Kuomintang government in Wuhan, and as he did so the governor of Hunan released his soldiers against the Communists there.

To be sure, the peasant with his bloodied scythe had behaved savagely in the rural revolt of the previous year, but the response of the army was beyond all reason. Tens of thousands were butchered in that appalling May—peasants, workers, students. And of the twenty-five thousand members of the Communist Party, it has been estimated that fifteen thousand died.

But the bloodshed among the rice fields turned into dragon's teeth. The peasants never forgot the slaughter or who had been the slaughterers. Many officers of the Kuomintang army, sickened by the butchery, went over to the Communists and took their regiments with them. Among these men were those who were to become the great generals of the Communist armies in the future: Lin Piao, Ho Lung, and Chu Teh.

In the midst of this horror the Communist Party, totally demoralized, made feeble appeals for moderation. Whatever Mao's inner feelings might have been, he supported these appeals. Throughout the summer he and his colleagues in the

Peasant Training Institute urged the peasants to be patient and to aid and trust the "People's Government" in Wuhan. But the government had neither the will nor the force to move against the new warlords who had risen under its banners, and, in any case, the days of collaboration between the Kuomintang and the Communist Party had come to an end. Even as the Communists were appealing for reason, the leader of the Kuomintang, Wang Ching-wei, was negotiating with Chiang for a reconciliation of government and army.

As Wang and Chiang grew closer, the Communist Party held its Fifth Congress. In an air of increasing unreality they debated what they should do. Incredible though it may seem, some, such as Ch'en, argued that they should continue to collaborate with the Kuomintang. Mao felt it would be viable only if the Communists staked their all on the peasants' revolt, still flickering across the ravaged fields of Hunan. After a series of bitter debates Ch'en and his group won the day. Mao was so discouraged that he stopped attending the Congress, for it was clear to him that following the Kuomintang without arms of their own was too much like the sheep following the butcher.

But the debates came to an end, for on July 15 the Kuomintang expelled all members of the Communist Party and left them to the mercies of the army.

Faced with this disaster, the Communists decided to try new tactics. Under the influence of Li Li-san it was decided that, although still declaring that the Communists supported the left Kuomintang, Communist troops and those sympathetic to them would rise in revolt against the rule of Chiang Kai-shek. The hope was that the insurrection, later called the Autumn Harvest Uprising, would trigger off a general rebellion, that Chiang would be deposed, that the Kuomintang would ally itself once more with the Communist Party, and that the National Revolution would proceed as Stalin wished.

The plan was that troops commanded by Chu Teh at Nanchang would seize that city and that other Communist forces would rise across the countryside, seizing provincial towns like Changsha. The Nanchang uprising took place on August 1, 1927. It is a day of immense significance for China. The army, which followed the Communists' plan, gave them for the first time an armed force of their own to counter the might of Chiang; the generals and officers who led the uprising were to be the leaders of the Red Army in the years to come. In China today August 1 is celebrated as Red Army Day and is the date on which the founding of the Chinese Army is celebrated, but in the weeks following the Nanchang revolt it would have taken a brave man to forecast a future for either the Communist Party or its army.

The army took Nanchang but could not hold it. Within five days it was in full retreat. With powerful, well-armed Kuomintang forces at its heels, the army marched away through Fukien until it reached Swatow on the coast north of Hong Kong. There it was driven off by Kuomintang troops and by gunfire from foreign gunboats and wandered off back into the wilderness of Fukien.

While this fiasco was taking place, Mao was in Hunan with orders to play his part in the insurrection. He had been given four regiments to attack Changsha; its seizure was supposed to be the detonator that would lead to a general revolution in Hunan led by the Communist Party. The flaw in this reasoning was that there were few Communists left in the province; the butchery of the previous May had seen to that. Consequently, Mao was expected to rely on a body that no longer existed. Obedient to his orders, however, Mao collected his troops and prepared his plans for the attack on Changsha.

We do not know directly how Mao felt as he prepared to lead his first military command, but as he drew his troops together, he wrote a poem—the first of his to survive—called "Changsha." Like many of Mao's poems, it is really a song, but not a confident one. Standing on the Hsiang River, in the cold of autumn, he looked at the mountains and forests on the horizon, seeing:

> Eagles cleave the air,
> Fish glide in the limpid deep;
> Under freezing skies a million
>   creatures contend in freedom.
> Brooding over this immensity,
> I ask, on this boundless land
> Who rules over man's destiny?

Asking this question, Mao remembered the days of his youth in Changsha, armed "with the scholar's bright blade and unafraid."

And now the pen had been put aside for the sword; the clearcut answers of youth had gone. Who would decide men's destinies in the days of fire ahead?

Mao planned to attack the city from three directions. As the Communist militia inside Changsha rose, his regular forces would storm the walls from outside. On September 9 Mao moved his troops forward. Striking from the north and the east, his regiments took their first objectives, but then ran into trouble. His Second Regiment was cut to pieces by superior forces, and the Fourth Regiment, deciding to return to the Kuomintang fold, turned on its allies and badly mauled the Third Regiment. But despite these losses Mao reached Changsha. Mao's plan had certain resemblances to the taking of Changsha by the New Army in 1911, but conditions now were not the same. Instead of a demoralized garrison the troops on the walls were tough and determined, and the militia had been mowed down by their machine guns. Mao and his troops hung around outside the walls for a time, but by September 15 he recognized defeat, and as the disastrous September ended, he marched away from Changsha, east, to the desolation of the mountains of Kiangsi.

The retreat was bitter, humiliating, and exhausting. Kuomintang armies barred the way to the mountains, and the Red troops had to fight a running battle for weeks on end. The ill-armed and outnumbered Communists were defeated repeatedly. Their casualty rate rose, and as the weather broke and food ran short, the soldiers, trudging through the rain, became more discouraged. Desertions became frequent, and discipline began to break down. The peasants, faced with what seemed to them no more than another marauding army, became hostile and refused aid. The commander of the ragged army himself went over to the Kuomintang. By the time winter came, it looked as if the army would disintegrate. But somehow the men held together. Those who stayed were the idealists, aware of what they were fighting for, and they were the bravest too. And in December, in drenching rain, barefoot, ragged, ill-fed, and ill-armed, they came to the clouded mountains of Chingkangshan.

ELEVEN

Chingkangshan rises on the border of Hunan, Kiangsi, and Kwangtung. It is a desolate area, remote and sparsely populated, a land of wild bush-covered mountains which for centuries have been the refuge of outlaws, rebels, runaways, fugitives from justice. In mountains such as these the heroes of Mao's favorite books had challenged the authority of the Emperor; and here, on Chingkangshan, as Mao led his battered remnant into its wilderness, they met, larger than life, two genuine bandit chiefs, Yuan Wen-ts'ai and Wang Tso.

The meeting of the Red soldiers and the wild and woolly bandits is as implausible as anything in a novel, and just as improbable is the fact that the two forces joined up—Yuan and Wang with six hundred men and a hundred and fifty rifles, Mao with a thousand soldiers, armed chiefly with revolutionary fervor.

In linking up with the bandits Mao was going against his party's orders. The Chinese Communist Party had a deep and not unjustified distrust of anyone who was not rooted in an identifiable social class. They relied on the workers and the peasants, whose revolutionary attitudes were guaranteed by their conditions of labor. Anyone outside the social order—thieves, bandits, beggars, prostitutes—they regarded as natural allies of the ruling class, which, indeed, had often used them to attack the working class, as in Shanghai in May.

As long ago as 1919, however, Mao had said that the revolution could find a place and a purpose for anyone, and now, on Chingkangshan, he was ready to use his bandit allies. Both men were made regimental commanders, and while the Red Army was on the mountain, they served it well. There was, in any case, a certain camaraderie between the two forces. After all, Red or bandit, the government was their common enemy. Also, and not to be overlooked, was the fact that Wang and Yuan were closely associated with the Ke Lao Hui, that secret society that in Mao's youth had led a revolt against the landowners of Shaoshan, and that was always intimately involved with the peasants.

Mao's headquarters in Chingkangshan was a deserted pagoda, and now, although he was at odds with his party and had been defeated in his first military command, and although from his pagoda he looked down on a China in the grip of his enemies, it is difficult not to believe that Mao was in his element. With his masters in the Communist Party far away, freed from the dogmas of Marxism, surrounded by men as rough and ready as himself, Mao was living the life of the heroes of his childhood, the bandits of the novel, *Water Margin*.

But the stay on Chingkangshan was not cakes and ale around a campfire. In the drenching rains of the winter there were eighteen hundred men who had to be fed and clothed and whose morale had to be maintained. For the bandits this was no real problem. They, after all, were bandits, whereas the Communists were there for a purpose, and not an ignoble one. The danger to them was that in their wretchedness and idleness they might degenerate, and instead of raising the bandits to their level be reduced to that of their allies.

This danger was one of which Mao and the Communist Party itself were keenly aware. To prevent this deterioration, to find an immediate and clear purpose for the troops, was a real challenge to Mao and his comrades on their mountain stronghold.

Mao's answer to the problem was simple and bold. He declared a people's government and declared Chingkangshan a self-governing district, independent of either the Kuomintang government in Wuhan or Chang Tso-lin's government in Peking. The state that Mao called into being was composed of five villages located at the five wells of the district. Its subjects were few and not all willing, and its armed forces outnumbered them. Still, the state, even if it was only the illusion of a state, existed. Laws were passed, the scanty land was redistributed among the peasants, the landlords and rich peasants were "reeducated," and, lest anyone should think the state too illusory, those who objected too strongly were executed.

The shooting of the landlords is a reminder that Mao and his men could be as ruthless as anyone else in China, and that men who carry guns intend to use them. Still, it is fair to say that the Communists were, relatively speaking, moderate men and that nothing like the inhuman savagery of the Shanghai and Hunan massacres took place under their rule. It is also possible to see the struggle of the Communists of Chingkangshan as a moral one. Their cause claimed to be one that would redeem China and lead mankind forward to a new era of unselfish freedom. The power they sought was not for themselves but so that this great cause could be brought to victory. How true this is, history will show, but certainly they believed it, there on the sodden mountains of Kiangsi.

In this struggle Mao was the standard-bearer. He was by no means alone. Other able men were with him, but it was Mao's gifts for compromise, for getting along with people, that held the men together. And not only Mao's gifts for leadership were tested during this winter. His self-confidence, too, was under pressure, for as the Communist Party learned of his actions it became increasingly critical of him.

In the eyes of the Central Committee Mao was guilty of a number of sins, and they regarded them as balefully as any inquisitor looking on a heresy. Mao was condemned for his retreat from Changsha, for joining up with Yuan and Wang, for "moderation"—that is, not killing enough landlords—and in particular for establishing a "base area," which in the opinion of the Central Committee led by Li Li-san meant a diversion of forces and energy from the all-important cities where, against all the evidence, they believed that the real revolution would take place—one day. For his sins Mao was deprived of all his posts in the party and was sent repeated messages ordering him to obey its directives. Mao's tactic for dealing with these orders was simple. If he disagreed with them, he ignored them.

This was easier for him to do than it might sound, for the Central Committee was now hiding in Shanghai, and by the time its messages reached the base they were often out of date. Doubly so, really, for the Central Committee was usually acting on decisions taken in Moscow, often months previously.

Mao did not ignore his superiors in Shanghai out of perversity. He was as dedicated to communism as they were, and an equally devout believer in Marx. But Chingkangshan brought out in him his greatest quality: the ability to face reality. In the mists of the mountains he could see, as the theoreticians in Shanghai could not, that the great revolution could not take place then, that he and his forces were too weak and isolated to do more than make guerrilla raids into the Kuomintang territory around his base, and that the only way to keep the cause alive was to build up his troops steadily and patiently, as steadily and patiently as the peasant tends his rice fields.

And throughout December and January, as his men lived on roots and water, Mao built up his small army. Men trickled into Chingkangshan—genuine revolutionaries, deserters from the Kuomintang, criminals on the run, bitter and resentful men driven from their farms, drifters and riffraff of all kinds. Mao took them all. "Everyone has his strong points. He should be encouraged to develop and put to good use those strong points, however limited they may be. Even the lame, the deaf, and the blind could all help in the revolutionary struggle."

As the men came in, Mao and his officers took them and searched for those points that could be developed. Rules were worked out that the slowest mind could grasp: prompt obedience to orders, no confiscations from poor peasants, all goods taken from rich peasants and landlords to be handed over promptly to the government. There was to be no excuse for theft or looting; no man could say that he did not know it was forbidden. Obedience to orders meant that the army remained a tight and controlled force. The political officers, the commissars, were always at the soldiers' elbows—exhorting, explaining, driving the revolutionary role of the army into the ears of the roughest recruit. And slowly the battered remnant of the Autumn Harvest Uprising was remolded into a serious revolutionary force.

But in the spring of 1928 Mao received new orders from Li Li-san. He was commanded to move from his base and march through south Hunan. Once again the theory was that the terror that the appearance of the Red troops would bring would start a revolutionary upsurge among the peasants. All China would be consumed in this revolution, and the Communist Party would sweep to power. The orders were categorical, and, short of leaving the party, Mao had to obey. Reluctantly he led the army from its base and marched east.

The move was nearly a disaster. The Kuomintang forces in Hunan swooped on the ill-armed, ill-trained army and cut it to pieces, and while it was away, the base of Chingkangshan was captured by government soldiers. Mao's position now was as bad as after the retreat from Changsha. Again he was wandering through a desolate countryside, his troops once more demoralized and cut off from any allies he might have. As he moved back into Kiansgi, he came across another Communist force: the army that had mutinied at Nanchang the previous autumn. After being driven from Swatow, they too had wandered into Kiangsi, and it was here that the army of Chingkangshan met them and their commanders, Chu Teh and Lin Piao.

Like the Nanchang uprising, the meeting of Mao and Chu is seen as a crucial moment in the making of modern China, and rightly so. From that union of forces were to come the leadership and the power that took the Communist Party—and Mao—to victory. But as Mao and Chu turned to Chingkangshan, they could foresee none of this, only a future dark, unpromising, and bloody.

How bloody the next weeks were to show. The Kuomintang troops were driven from the mountains, but, reinforced, they turned again to strike at the Communists. Week after week they attacked, outgunning and outnumbering the Red Army. To survive at all, Mao and Chu and Lin Piao had to evolve new ways of fighting. Instead of being drawn into stand-up fights, they learned to run when outnumbered and to attack again only when they had overwhelming superiority. Once again the Communists worked out simple rules for their soldiers, rules so simple that they could be painted in only four characters each, which made a little verse:

When the enemy advances, we retreat.
When the enemy retreats, we advance.
When the enemy rests, we harass him.
When the enemy avoids a battle, we attack.

But tactics like these do not succeed because they are militarily correct: the fighting men must be ready and able to move at high speed without losing discipline, either advancing or, much more difficult, retreating. They also need the ability to act independently when contact with officers is lost, and to maintain complete trust between man and man.

The infant Red Army was learning these qualities, but in May Li Li-san once more sent emissaries to the base with orders to invade Hunan again. This time Mao was pushed into disobeying the order. He called a meeting and denounced the Central Committee for this act of folly. His meeting, however, was held away from the base of the army, and while he was absent, Chu was ordered directly to march. And he went.

Stripped of its troops, Chingkangshan was again an obvious target for the Kuomintang. As Chu Teh led his army through Hunan, the base was attacked again. With a handful of men Mao held off the enemy for twenty-five days, but as the fourth week began, the Kuomintang soldiers had gnawed their way into the heart of the base. By the end of August it was clear that the end was in sight. Leaing his men, Mao slipped through the Kuomintang lines in darkness and went in search of Chu Teh.

At Kueiting, in south Hunan, Mao found the army. Half of it had been lost, either in battle or by desertion, but those who remained were willing to return to the base. By now, except for a few hilltops held by small groups of men, the base was entirely under Kuomintang control. Months of hard fighting were necessary to take Chingkangshan again, but by the end of 1928 Mao and the Communists were once more masters of their base. And they were to become even stronger, for later on a commander of the Kuomintang regiment came over to the Communists, bringing his regiment with him. But success brought its own problems. The mountain base could not grow enough crops to support such large numbers of men. For months they lived on squash. Few of the men had winter clothes. They shivered in the mists, taking as their slogan, "Down with the landlords—and live on squash!"

But good humor will not stave off hunger, and in January it was clear that the base would have to be evacuated. It was not only the food supply that dictated the move. The base was still under heavy attack, and although the army was defeating its enemy, a mood of depression was sweeping through the troops. Sitting on the mountains was not spreading the revolutionary gospel, and those to whom they did preach it were not responsive. "Everywhere," Mao wrote, "the masses are cold and aloof . . . enemy troops do not desert to us, and there are hardly any cases of mutiny on their side."

In this mood of depression the revolutionary army moved off the mountain, leaving Wang behind, and struck south to Tungku in Kiangsi. At a town called Tapoti the troops were caught by a big Kuomintang army and fought a terrible battle in which they lost half their strength. The rest slashed their way clear and reached Tungku. Left to his own devices, Wang returned to his banditry and was killed by the peasants.

The army was now relatively safe, but its morale had suffered during the retreat. Mao noted among the soldiers a reluctance to settle down, a love of change and movement. Theft and disobedience became more common. Worst of all, the habits of the Kuomintang army, from which most of the men had come, began to reassert themselves, with officers beating men and the men becoming surly and slipshod. Now the danger to the army was from within and the challenge to its leaders more formidable because of that.

But as the army settled in its new base and conditions improved, so did its morale; the veterans of Chingkangshan hardened again into a tight, determined, and disciplined force. In Kiangsi, too, the peasants were more welcoming than in the north, and as they responded to the Communists' program of reform, the army began to believe in its revolutionary role again.

However, although Mao and Chu Teh looked with satisfaction on their new base and the increasingly formidable army they were creating, in Shanghai the Central Committee was still restless about Mao's strategy. The Committee, led by Li Li-san, still refused to believe that the revolution could take place unless it was led by the industrial working class of the cities. Rural base areas such as the one in Kiangsi, although useful in helping to build up armies, could mean only diversion of effort from the all-important industrial areas. Accordingly, in April, Li wrote to Mao ordering him to break up the army and send its units out in groups into the countryside. In this way, Li believed, the flame of revolt would be kept alive in the countryside without its dominating the "real" revolution.

Mao noted the letter and, in fact, wrote back agreeing with it, but he did not obey it. Instead, he and Chu set about organizing an even bigger base. Indeed, Mao's confidence had now been restored to the point where he was thinking of building up an army that would—on its own—conquer the whole of Kiangsi province without reference to the cities at all. Events in Kiangsi helped to confirm him in this belief. The Red Army, led by absolutely outstanding commanders, such as Chu Teh, Lin Piao, Ho Lung, and Peng Teh-huai, made mincemeat of the Kuomintang armies that hung around the base. So confident was Mao of his strength that he declared the base a "soviet area," meaning a self-governing state inside China, and organized on the Russian model of "soviets," or people's councils.

Although Mao could sit in Kiangsi and survey with haughty satisfaction the strength and security of his base, new orders were about to reach him which he could not ignore. In the spring of 1930 it seemed as if the global system of capitalism were about to disintegrate and, with its fall, shatter the anti-Communist forces inside China and bring about the real revolution.

TWELVE

From the end of the war until 1929 the Western economies had enjoyed a remarkable boom. Production and consumption had risen rapidly. But for reasons not fully understood then—any more than inflation is understood now—a huge crisis shook the West. The goods the factories produced were not bought, unemployment soared, and in the midst of unimaginable wealth a third of the population of the developed countries slid into poverty. The result of this distress was violence, strikes and riots, and insurrection. Since the birth of capitalism the West had suffered a cycle of slump and boom; now, it appeared, it was in a slump from which it could not recover. In the nineteenth century Karl Marx had prophesied such a collapse and had declared that it would be the final crisis of capitalism. After it would come either the end of civilization or communism.

Communists all over the world had awaited the Final Crisis of Capitalism. Now, they thought, it had come, and it was the duty of all Communists to attack the disintegrating system, destroying it so that they would be free to build a new and better world.

This is what the Russians thought; it was what Li Li-san thought, too. Urged on by the Russians to play his part in bringing about the new world, he ordered a general attack on all Kuomintang forces in China, particularly the cities, and

more particularly the cities of the Yangtze Basin. The armies
that were to do this attacking were the armies of the soviet
base of Kiangsi.

In June Li Li-san sent out his orders, orders Mao could not
ignore. In August the Red Army marched from the base in
three columns, ready to do its part in shattering the capitalist
system. The army was led by three generals of the highest
caliber: Peng, who was to attack Changsha; the great Ho
Lung, whose target was Wuhan; and Chu Teh, who, with
Mao, was to capture Nanchang. Peng took the much battered
Changsha but could not hold it and was forced to retreat.
Falling back from the city, he contacted the army of Chu
Teh and Mao, which had been badly beaten at Nanchang.
During Peng's retreat he had received new orders from Li
Li-san, instructing him to attack Changsha yet again, using
Chu's army as a reinforcement. Once more the armies attacked the city. For thirteen days, under bombardment from
the air and from gunboats on the river, they threw themselves
at the walls. But the struggle was hopeless. On the thirteenth
day Mao, on his own responsibility and against orders, called
off the battle and led the army away from the city, back to
the mountains of Chingkangshan. Behind him he left thousands of dead and, inside the city, his wife, Yang K'ai-hui,
and his sister, Mao Tse-hung, both of whom, in a vile act of
revenge, were beheaded by the governor.

And so the great offensive had failed, and once again Mao
had defied his superiors. But, as before, it was they and not
he who vanished from the seat of power. As Ch'en, after his
errors, had been called to face the inquisitors of Moscow, so
now Li Li-san received his summons. But as Li left, taking
with him the dogmas of 1930, new emissaries arrived from
the U.S.S.R., bringing with them the dogmas of 1931.

The new men, whom the Soviets intended to lead the
Chinese Communist Party, were men whom the Comintern
delegates in China had selected for training in the Soviet
Union. Known ironically as the "Returned Students," or the
"Twenty-Eight Bolsheviks," and led by a Soviet adviser, Pavel
Mif, and a completely inexperienced Chinese, Wang Ming,
they were as ignorant of the conditions in China as the Sovi-
ets themselves, but they did not allow this to inhibit them.
Once they had established themselves in Shanghai, they were
to become locked in a struggle with Mao for the leadership

of the Communist Party, which only near disaster would resolve.

Mao was busy re-establishing the base area in Kiangsi as the "students" settled down. He laid enormous stress on training the troops, giving them not only military but political instruction, ensuring that every man knew not only how to fight but what he was fighting for. Priority number two was the organization of the economic life in the soviet. If the soviet was to survive against its enemies, it must have the support of the population within it—not all of whom by any means were pro-Communist. Consequently, the Communists were extremely moderate in their treatment of even the fairly well-to-do peasants. By these methods Mao was hoping to build up a base from which, in times to come, the Red Army would be strong enough to strike out at its enemies. The real argument between Mao and Li Li-san was not the long-term aim of defeat of the Kuomintang, but at what time it should be attempted. For Mao the time had not yet come.

Moa's moderation, sensible though it was, was not accepted by all the Communists of the Kiangsi Soviet. Still believing in the theories of Li Li-san, a group of his supporters called a meeting and denounced Mao's policy as anti-Marxist and anti-revolutionary. Mao promptly arrested the leaders of the meeting, whereupon the 20th Army, from whose ranks the critics came, rose up in revolt against him. And Mao struck back.

So far we have seen Mao as a moderate and balanced man, holding power but using it as gently as possible. The revolt of the 20th Army, however, brought out all Mao's ruthlessness. In brief but ferocious attack he broke the revolt and showed no mercy to its leaders or its followers. It has been estimated that as many as three thousand men died in this bloody affair, and when it was over there was no doubt who was master in Kiangsi or what manner of man he was. Mao had undoubtedly an attractive personality—his blend of unassuming peasant and artist, his engaging personality with its odd dreaminess and friendliness, made him a man one could like and respect. But behind the personality was a will of steel which, in the last resort, would allow no challenge to its cause. And, to be sure, as Mao ground the rebels into the earth, he must have had with him the thought of his wife and sister, headless in the dust of Changsha.

As Mao disposed of his enemies inside the base, a new enemy appeared from the outside. Tired of the hornets' nest at his rear, Chiang sent an army down to Kiangsi to wipe it out, in what was called the First Encirclement Campaign. Although outnumbered two to one, and ill-armed, the Red Army, using the guerrilla tactics learned on Chingkangshan, slashed the Kuomintang forces to ribbons. Within two months Chiang was forced to withdraw his army, but like a snake it recoiled, only to strike again. In the spring of 1931 the Kuomintang army, heavily reinforced, attacked once more. Again it was defeated, and this time the shock brought Chiang himself down from his new capital of Nanking. Taking personal control of the army, now numbering half a million men, he launched the Third Encirclement Campaign against the forty thousand men of the Red Army.

Chiang's campaign began with what seemed to be a series of successes. Almost unopposed, his columns moved into the Red base until he was deep in its heart. Then, with its enemies far from their supply depots and surrounded by a hostile population, the Red troops struck. Using their superb mobility, the Communists slashed and sliced the Kuomintang until, bleeding to death, Chiang was forced once more to retreat. By August he had clearly lost the battle, by September he was pulling his regiments from the line, and in October he had withdrawn totally.

The defeat of the three campaigns was a triumph for the battle plans of Mao and Chu Teh, but it was not only those plans that had forced Chiang to retreat. There was another reason and another threat, this time from overseas.

Japan, still casting its long shadow over China, was increasingly using its army to dictate policy to the Emperor's government. On September 18 officers of the Japanese Army blew up a train on which Chang Tso-lin, the ex-master of the Peking government, was traveling, and used the incident as a pretext for seizing the city of Mukden, thus effectively taking control of Manchuria and threatening north China. It was to deal with this menace that Chiang hurried north.

The success of Mao in defending the Kiangsi base had, of course, been noted by the party leadership, still leading a dangerous underground existence in Shanghai. Although opposed to Mao's tactics, the Central Committee, now dominated by the "Returned Students," was ready to take advantage of the security the base offered, and in September it decided to leave Shanghai and transfer to Kiangsi. The appearance of the "Returned Students" was the signal for another struggle for power inside the base. The Central Committee, led now by Wang Ming, still believed that Mao, with his stress on the importance of the countryside, was leading the Communist Party away from the industrial proletariat, and thus away from the only genuine communist revolution.

With the Central Committee actually in the base, Mao could no longer ignore its orders as he had been in the habit of doing. Furthermore, Wang made it clear that Mao was to have his power curbed. He lost control of the army, which was given to Chou En-lai, and although Mao was made Chairman of the Council of People's Commissars, this was a post without real authority. Increasingly, Mao was pushed further into the shadows.

Having taken control of the soviet, Wang and his allies declared a new policy. No longer would the Red Army use its guerrilla tactics in battle, nor would the Communist Party move slowly, increasing the size of the base by a steady enlargement of its borders. Instead, as in the days of Li Li-san, there would be a bold forward policy, with the army marching forth to attack the enemy in frontal assaults.

Throughout the summer this policy was carried out with spectacular results. The base was increased in size until it was almost as large as France and Germany together, and its population was more than three million. Unchallenged, the Red Army marched where it willed, and now, because of the surrender of two Kuomintang army brigades with all their weapons, it was for the first time adequately armed.

While the Red Army enjoyed its summer of glory, and while Wang's new policy was to all appearances correct, Mao was occupied with the comparatively humdrum tasks of organizing the economy of the base, doomed now, it seemed, to a future as a second-rate and unimportant administrator. But what neither Wang nor any of his allies noticed was that the Red Army was unchallenged only because there was no army near enough to oppose them, and that their main enemy, Chiang Kai-shek, was leaving them alone only in order to deal with the continuing problem of the Japanese.

Certainly Chiang had his hands full. Following their seizure of Manchuria, the Japanese had turned on Shanghai. Trumping up an excuse about ill-treatment of Japanese citizens, they attacked the forts that guarded the port, thus hoping to gain control of the Yangtze River, the key to the mastery of central China. Contemptuous of the Chinese, Japan expected a quick victory. But China had changed. No longer were the Chinese cowed by the sight of a gunboat; the 19th Army defended the city with incredible heroism. Eventually an agreement was patched up between Chiang and the Japanese, and the Kuomintang general was free to turn again to the maddening rebels of Kiangsi.

At the base, Chiang's return was expected. Wang Ming had returned to Moscow, but his place had been taken by Po Ku, another "Returned Student" and one convinced that Wang was correct. Following Wang, Po Ku and the Central Committee had prepared new plans for meeting this attack. Instead of using Mao's tactics of the previous campaign—luring the enemy into hostile territory and then cutting it to pieces—the Red Army was going to meet Chiang outside the gates of the base. This time, as Wang had put it, their pots and pans would be broken.

Mao, ill with malaria, isolated from the army, and in disgrace with his party, argued against this policy but was overruled. In the tremendous struggle that was to come he had to sit on the sidelines—and watch the Red Army inflict on Chiang a crushing defeat.

Chiang came down from the north with half a million men and within three months was totally defeated. The Red Army, meeting him head-on, broke his crack regiments, captured his commanders, looted his equipment, and inflicted on Chiang what he admitted to be the greatest humiliation of his life.

As Chiang marched the remnants of his army away, the Communists were jubilant. At last they had an army which need not hide away in the hills but which was capable of taking on the most powerful forces in China in open combat. With such an army the "right" Kuomintang could be smashed and the Communists could then return to their alliance with the "left" Kuomintang and bring about, perhaps in the near future, the triumph of the Revolution.

Event after event helped to confirm the Central Committee in this view. Other soviets were being established across

China, many beyond the reach of Chiang, and outside the soviet areas the Communist Party was recovering from the disasters of the slaughters of 1927. And, as well, and in the long run more important, among many otherwise nonpolitical Chinese there was a growing discontent with Chiang. As in the days of the Emperor, men were beginning to ask themselves what the use was of leaders who could not defend China against attack from the outside. And all Chiang's arguments that the Communists were a greater menace to China than Japan were met with a cold indifference. After all—and nothing could alter the fact—the Communists were Chinese. It was feelings like these that in 1933 led to the revolt of the 19th Army and the establishment of another independent government in China. With such developments the Communists could well feel confident and cheerfully greet the news that Chiang was preparing once more to attack them.

But now the tide turned. Chiang destroyed the 19th Army, signed a treaty with the Japanese, brought the rest of the warlords to his heels, and in October came again to Kiangsi.

This time, although such figures are hard to credit, Chiang had an army of a million soldiers, and in addition to the ocean of men, he brought new plans and new advisers. At his elbows were two German generals, Hans von Seeckt and Ludwig von Falkenhausen. Both these men had learned their trade in the slaughterhouse of World War I. They were masters of static warfare, and this was what Chiang intended to use against the Kiangsi Soviet in his Fifth Encirclement Campaign.

His campaign began in October 1933. It started not with swaggering advances into the heart of the Red Base but with slow and laborious building. His army was equipped with shovels as well as rifles, concrete as well as bullets, and his men used them to build a ring of blockhouses. Each of these small forts was covered by its neighbor with machine-gun fire, the space between them was blocked with barbed wire, and the wire had artillery ranged on it.

From November through February the ring was built. In the spring the soviet "government" announced that it would cooperate with anyone and any force that would end the Civil War. Whether this appeal was sincere or not, it had no meaning, for outside Chiang's "walls of fire" no one could hear it. Inside the base, as the months went by, conditions became worse. Food, salt, and medicine ran short. Every day Chiang's planes roamed the sky, bombing with impunity, and his heavy guns, unanswered, shelled far into the area. The Red Army, following the dictates of Wang, attacked the Kuomintang in open combat, seeking to relive the victories of the Fourth Campaign, but, in Mao's phrase, they merely "milled" about between the blockhouses and Chiang's main forces and were shot to pieces by his artillery and machine guns. It was, as Mao said, a "stupid way to fight"—stupid, suicidal, and disastrous. Nothing could break Chiang's grip; and the unquestioned courage of the Communist troops was meaningless against his firepower.

The summer drew near, and still there was no respite. As the military situation deteriorated without any sign of a coherent strategy from the Central Command, morale slipped. Bitter quarrels broke out among the defenders. The peasants, alarmed for their future, grew colder to the Communists; guerrillas, sent in by Chiang, organized the old landlords' militia and sabotaged roads and bridges. By the end of the summer it had become clear that the base could no longer be held. The Red Army would have to break out of the "walls of fire" and abandon the Kiangsi Soviet.

But where was the army to go? The plans of the Central Committee were confused and contradictory, but from the welter of debate one suggestion began to gain acceptance. The soviet base in Hunan was controlled by Ho Lung and the Second Front Army. If the Red Army could get there and join him with his fresh and confident troops, there would be time to think again about the future prospects of the Chinese Communist Party. This plan, or, rather, vague hope, for it was never thoroughly worked out, was the best that the Central Committee could propose. In October the troops were concentrated in the northeast corner of the base, and on October 14 ninety thousand men struck at the Kuomintang line.

THIRTEEN

Four lines of fortifications faced the Red Army. The first, which was the weakest, was swept aside without difficulty. Ten days later the second line was breached, and a week later the third was broken, but only after ferocious fighting. By October 29 the last line had been swept aside and the army was in the open.

Through the gap that the vanguard had cleared came the rest of the army and with it the baggage of the base—the records of the Kiangsi Soviet, the treasury, machinery, printing presses, and what simple medical supplies the Communists had—all defended by the rearguard—crack troops whose job it was to stop the enemy striking at the vast migration. Left behind in the base were the sick and the wounded, women, and children—including three of Mao's who were never recovered—protected by a cloud of guerrilla fighters, among them Mao's brother, Mao Tse-t'an, who was killed in action. Some women went on the March, among them Chu Teh's indomitable wife, K'ang K'e-ch'ing, carrying three rifles when she did not have a wounded soldier across her back, and Mao's new wife, Ho Tzu-chen, who was pregnant.

Free from the "walls of fire," the Red Army swung northwest and struck a line for Szechwan. Throughout November and December it marched across Kwangtung and Kwangsi provinces, and with every mile it marched it left its dead behind. Its unswerving route made it easy for the Kuomintang generals to foresee where it would be at any given time and to throw their armies across its path. The Red Army, fighting with the energy of demons, broke every attack, but still the losses mounted. As December dawned and the army moved into Kweichow, the rains came, turning the roads into mud and slowing the pace of the troops. The endless lines of baggage carriers lagged farther and farther behind, stretching the line of protective troops ever thinner, making it easy for the Kuomintang to strike at their flanks.

Halfway through December the army came to the Hsiang River. If the route to the north was to be continued, the river had to be crossed. The Kuomintang had the river covered and it had to be crossed in an inferno of fire. After suffering heavy losses, the army forced a bridgehead, and after another week's heavy fighting the army managed to cross the river. Coming after weeks of heavy fighting and nonstop skirmishing, the battle of the river had seriously weakened the army, exhausted and dispirited it. The battered troops slumped on the muddy bank of the Hsiang River had been fighting now for five months, and fighting and marching for another two months. Behind them lay the bloodstained miles of the road from Kiangsi; ahead of them lay army after army—rested, fed, well-armed, merely waiting for the Red Army to walk onto their bayonets. Wang had led them to this pass, but as the shadow of defeat began to fall across him and his supporters, from their darkness came other men, and leading them was Mao.

For six years Mao had led the army of rural China, and in those years he had gathered a motley collection of peasants, vagabonds, and deserters and built them into a powerful and dedicated army. Under him the army had seen itself growing in strength, secure in its base, and victorious over the Kuomintang. Now, after Mao had been excluded from the leadership and deprived of high military command, the troops found themselves forced from their base, battered to pieces by the enemy, and stranded on the Hsiang River without either base or objective. Licking its wounds, the army looked again to Mao, and under his pressure the plan to strike directly at Szechwan was dropped. The army turned, instead, to the west, to Kweichow, where the enemy was weak and unprepared.

Shaken but undaunted, the army rose to its feet and re-crossed the Hsiang. Now it marched light: the printing presses were abandoned, the machines buried; every man took what he could carry and nothing else. The pressure of events was turning the Red Army away from its assumed role of a modern, conventional army and back to its guerrilla function. Back, in fact, to its origins, for on the Chingkangshan the army had been born as a quick-moving force whose strength lay, not in that regimented and technical might that wins set-piece battles, but in the loose and speedy cuts of the swordsman.

The army was split into columns—two, three, four—and the columns, freed from the weight of the baggage train, darted across the hills of Kweichow. Like an irate man trying to swat a fly, the Kuomintang armies struck, and struck again, only to find the Red Army gone. Now the big guns of Chiang boomed in vain, and his black bombers droned over empty hills.

Then, just as the Red Army had melted into the landscape, it reappeared, its morale soaring, to strike back. In central Kweichow it came to the River Wu. Across the river, sited on a cliff, was a fort. It looked impregnable, the crossing impossible. But at night a handful of men crossed the river, stormed the cliffs, and took the fort. In January, looking for a much-needed center where it could rest, the army came to Tsunyi, the provincial capital of Kweichow. Carrying captured Kuomintang banners, the troops knocked on the gates and were welcomed by the garrison as much-needed reinforcements, a mistake recognized by the governor only when his palace was occupied by the Central Committee.

The capture of Tsunyi gave the army a breathing space. The nearest Kuomintang forces were miles away, floundering in the winter's mud, and presented no immediate danger. Now, as the wounded and the stragglers came in and the men rested after their thousand-mile journey, was the time to reappraise the whole concept of the March. The leadership called, or was pushed into calling, a conference on the future plans of the Red Army—a conference that was to be the final and crucial fight for the leadership of the Chinese Communist Party.

The first priority of the conference was the future, but there were also the events of the past weeks to debate. The army, although it had escaped Chiang's noose, had nonetheless suffered very heavy losses, as many as thirty thousand men, and it was clear that this was a result of the head-on tactics the army had been ordered to apply. Mao was free from blame for this decision, and when the conference looked at the ruin of the soviet and at the position of the army it threw out the old leaders and made Mao Chairman of the Politburo—in fact, if not in name, the supreme leader of both party and army.

The debate over the leadership of the party was the result of long-standing differences between rival groups and was carried out in standard Marxist phraseology, much of it meaningless to non-Marxists. Even now a mystery surrounds the actual details of the conference. But behind the Marxist jargon, with its appeals to "historical inevitability" and "bourgeois contradictions," was an appeal to the final tribunal of the Red Army.

On the men who made the army, on their discipline and stamina, their bravery and beliefs, lay the future of the Communist Party. Many of them were barely literate, able to read only a few characters; some had been bandits. Most of them had come from the rice fields, leaving their hoes and picking up rifles. No matter what eloquence might be unleashed, no matter what mastery of Marxist dialectics demonstrated, whoever led the Red Army in the future would have to hold the loyalty, affection, and trust of these hard-bitten men. Darkened by sun and wind, barefoot, ragged, carrying a rifle over one shoulder and a tattered umbrella over the other, they thought their own thoughts, squatting in the dust outside the palace of the governor of Kweichow as their leaders debated their future inside it.

There was only one man for the army: Mao Tse-tung. When Mao had gained control of the party, the army was with him and for him, ready to follow him even to his goal, Yenan in Shensi province, two thousand miles away to the north.

For at last, after the wanderings of the past months, the army had a purpose. During the conference many plans had been put forward for the next move of the army, most of them vague or impracticable. But Mao now showed his real genius. Looking forward, not merely in terms of months or years, but decades, he advocated marching to the remoteness of the Shensi Soviet area to fight, not the Kuomintang, but the Japanese.

The boldness of this decision is not easy to appreciate at first. But think of the Red Army in the subtropical forest of Kweichow, and then think of the vast arid lands of Shensi. Think, also of the two thousand miles of desolation between them, and realize that the only way to cover those miles was to walk. Bear in mind that at the end of the March would not be a comfortable rest area but a few villages in the most backward part of China, an area hardly touched by civilization, and that waiting for the army in Manchuria, across the border, were the murderous armies of the Japanese.

But that is merely the physical aspect of the plan. Its true greatness lay in the fact that Mao had seen that the battle against the Japanese—with which China was not then even at war—would be the arena in which the mastery of China would be decided. This tremendous insight—and it was a visionary insight—sprang not from Marxism or theories dreamed up by the West, but directly from Mao's true identification of himself and his party with China. In the secondary struggle—the bitter conflict between Chiang and the Communist Party—it would be the party, seen most clearly by the Chinese peopple to be defending China, that would win.

The first step in carrying out this strategy was to reach the north. At first Mao intended to cross the Yangtze east of Chungking, but during the stay at Tsunyi Chiang had marshaled his armies to cut off any move the Communists might make in that direction, and other hostile forces were already near the city. Once more Mao divided his forces and unleashed his columns. For months the army marched and countermarched across Kweichow, throwing the Kuomintang forces into confusion. As Chiang's men floundered in the mud, the Red soldiers chopped at them from the shelter of the bamboo forests. When the Kuomintang troops counterattacked, the Communists disappeared. It was like fighting ghosts, but ghosts armed with bullets.

Not all the battles were guerrilla raids. In March Mao called his columns together and swept north to the Kweichow-Szechwan border, and there in the mountains, at

Louchang Pass, in bitter frost, they shattered the army of the military governor of Kweichow. As the Red Army stood on the summit of the pass, with all Szechwan province lying before it, wild geese cried overhead, flying into the icy clarity of the northern skies. But the Red Army did not follow the birds. Mao called his men away from Szechwan—and the armies of Chiang Kai-shek waiting there—and went south, down to Tsunyi, across the Wu River, deep into Kweichow, straight at the town of Kueiyang, where Chiang had established his headquarters in his pursuit of the Communists.

Staggered at the approach of his terrible foe, Chiang frantically called in his troops from Yunnan province to the west, whereupon Mao swung away from Kueiyang and into the undefended province. Moving at astonishing speed, the Red Army stabbed down at Yunnanfu, the provincial capital, where Chiang's wife was hurriedly catching a train to French Indo-China. As the Kuomintang armies splashed south through the wild rain forests, the Red Army was cheerfully marching north, and this time Mao intended to follow the wild geese.

The Red Army was heading for a crossing on the Yangtze River, called the Golden Sand River, which was the entrance to Szechwan. Had Chiang himself given the orders to his enemy he could not have wished for anything more satisfactory. The Golden Sand River is a savage, turbulent stream, roaring down a huge gorge as it spills from the edge of the Himalayas. There are no bridges, and there are no fords. The only way to cross is by ferryboat, and Chiang had ordered that every boat on the river be destroyed. As the Red Army marched to the river, Chiang's troops marched behind it, confident that the Communists would be trapped against the river and annihilated.

Shadowed by Chiang's planes, the Red Army reached Louchang Ferry and began building a bridge. Now Chiang could sleep easy; the bridge-building would take weeks, and long before then he would have Mao by the throat. But unknown to the Kuomintang, a troop of Red soldiers was already on its way to Chou Ping ferry, eighty-five miles downstream. It took the men twenty-four hours to cover the distance. Dressed as Kuomintang troops, they hailed the opposite bank, calling for a boat. The garrison on the other side obligingly sent one over, the Red troops rowed across—and the crossing was secure. The main army, which had finished playacting at the bridge at Louchang, made a forced march downstream and appeared the next day. Nine days later the army was over the river and striking into Szechwan. There is no record of what happened to the Kuomintang officer who did not burn his boats—nor to the men who told the Red Army that the boats were there.

Once again the Red Army had slipped from the grasp of the Kuomintang, but once again, it seemed, it was heading for disaster. As the Communists padded north across the mountains of Ta Hsueh Shan, three miles an hour, twelve hours out of twenty-four, the forces of the Kuomintang were gathering once more. Behind them came the army of Hunan; on their right flank, shadowing them across the Yangtze, were the armies of Szechwan, and ahead of them was a barrier more formidable than even the Golden Sand: the Tatu River.

Ta Hsueh Shan and the Tatu River have evil memories for Chinese insurrectionists. Rebel after rebel has been maneuvered into its gorges and destroyed, and here the Taiping army had met its end at the hands of the great imperial general, Tseng Kuo-fan. There is no escape. The river cannot be crossed against opposition, and there is only one exit from the trap, toward the desolation of Tibet. There, on the roof of the world, only death from starvation awaits the refugee. And there is one more thing:

West Szechwan, at the very rim of China, is the home of the Lolo tribe. Warlike and unconquered even by the greatest of the Chinese Emperors, the Lolo tribesmen were traditional enemies of the Chinese. No army could pass through their territory without fierce fighting. If the Red Army ever did arrive at the Tatu, it would be exhausted and decimated. Well might the generals of the Kuomintang feel that at last the Communists had been delivered into their hands. But they reckoned without the ingenuity of their opponents. The Communist generals sat with the Lolo chieftains and drank cock's blood with them; the soldiers gave them rifles and bullets; the commissars promised them protection against the Szechwan mercenaries. When the Red troops came down from the great mountains, they were led by Lolo guides, who brought them down to the crossing of Anshunchang. And there, below them, as they looked down on the gorge of the Tatu and the river roaring through it, they saw on the north

bank three ferryboats. They also saw something else. On their
side of the river was another boat.

The boat belonged to an unwise general who was visiting
relatives. The Red scouts swooped down and captured general and boat. Using the boat, a handful of volunteers crossed
the river under heavy fire and took the Kuomintang fort
guarding the crossing. The way was now open for the army
to cross the river, but a force intervened that even the Red
Army could not control.

Away on the gigantic plateau of Tibet the snows were
melting, and the rivers of China, fed by their waters, were
rising in the spring floods. The waters of the Tatu rose in a
huge spate. It became an almost impossible task to get the
ferryboats over the river. On the south bank, as the main
body of the army came to the crossing, an enormous traffic
jam built up. Chiang's planes spotted the army and bombed
it; his armies were drawing nearer, and each hour brought
the fate of the Taiping army closer to the sixty thousand men
of the Red Army.

Faced with disaster, twenty-six-year-old Lin Piao, leader of
the vanguard, called an emergency conference. Mao, Chou
En-lai, and the generals, Chu Teh and Peng Teh-huai, sat
with him with the fate of the army in their hands. From
scouts they knew that a hundred miles up the river, at the
town of Luting, there was a bridge. If they could capture that
bridge, the army could escape. If not . . .

The divided army, a third on the north bank, the rest on
the south, began to move upstream, abandoning the ferry.
Ahead of it went the best troops the Red Army had, men
chosen for their stamina and dedication. They were given
three days to cover the hundred miles—days and nights, for
there was no rest. The way to Luting was along paths cut
into the gorges. The paths rose and fell so that men might
climb a thousand feet in half a mile, one minute finding
themselves above the roar of the river and its mist, the next
struggling knee-deep in its waters. On the second day, after
twenty miles had been covered, the soldiers were told to
speed their pace. Enemy troops had appeared on the north
bank, heading for the bridge. The troops were given twenty-
four hours to cover the next eighty miles.

The vanguard doubled their pace, trotting, running by
torchlight along the gorges. There was no rest. "Victory was

life," said Peng Teh-huai, "defeat death for us all." Men slipped and fell into the river, but there was no backward glance for them. Behind the vanguard the army crawled along the gorge. Long afterward men remembered the light of their torches—ten, twenty, thirty thousand of them—flaring in the deep blackness of the gorges. And on the morning of May 25 the Red troops came to the bridge of Luting.

The bridge had been built in the eighteenth century by a builder called Lin. Across the river, a hundred yards wide here, he had flung thirteen huge chains and anchored them in rock. Across the chains wooden planks made a safe, if unnerving, crossing. The troops guarding the bridge had pulled up half the planking, but in their casual and unhurried way they had left half of it down. On the north bank, where the town of Luting huddled under its tiled roofs, a guardhouse covered the bridge with machine guns.

It takes an Olympic champion more than nine seconds to cover a hundred yards. If the Red troops were to capture the bridge, they would have to cover that distance swinging on chains over a huge river, carrying weapons—and in the mouths of the enemy's guns. It was a job for volunteers, and thirty were chosen. Armed with automatic weapons, revolvers, and swords, and under a hail of covering fire from their comrades, early in the afternoon of May 26 the assault troops moved out onto the bridge.

The first men were cut down and plunged into the brown waters of the river, but behind them other men edged out along the chains. Inch by inch they crept out over the river. In the middle the bridge's curve made it harder for the Kuomintang machine guns to bear on them, and the rifle fire was too wild to be effective. By now the Red soldiers were near enough to strike back, and they lobbed grenades at the fort. But the Kuomintang troops had a card left to play. They poured paraffin on the planking and set fire to it. Ironically, the smoke from the fire gave cover for the Communists, and under it they dashed through the flames and stormed the fort. The Kuomintang troops fled, and the Red troops held the bridge.

Across the Tatu, the Red Army now marched north again. There was no pursuit. Chiang's armies reached the Tatu and halted, exhausted, out-generaled, and fought to a standstill.

Only Chiang Kai-shek flew over the Tatu in one of his

black planes. For hours he flew over the Red columns, looking down on the men who, hated and despised by him, had defied him for five years and who now, against all probability, had marched two thousand miles through his territory, defeating all he had sent against them, dressing themselves in his clothes, eating his food, shooting with his guns and his ammunition. As dusk darkened the purple mountains, he wheeled away to the south, while below him, marching relentlessly onward to its victory of victories, the Red Army struck north.

Although the Red Army was now safe from Chiang's guns, ahead lay an enemy mightier and, because impersonal, more daunting: the wilderness of mountains that form the western bastion of China. On these bare hills, where the wind blows forever, there was no call for volunteers, for no bravery was required—only the brute stamina of the ox, and that steadiness of heart more demanding than the warrior's rage.

Here men who had come unscathed through a hundred battles began to die of weariness, lying down under the western sky and marching no more. They died on the crossing of the Maanshan Pass, ten thousand feet high, and they died among the rhododendrons and bamboos at its foot. Beyond Maanshan they died on the ice peaks of the Chiachin Mountains, their bodies resting forever in the snows, seventeen thousand feet above their homeland.

After Chiachin there were more mountains—range after range, all cut by roaring rivers, and all to be climbed, all to be crossed, and all claiming their victims. Those who survived, those who marched on and on, making their own roads, building their own bridges—those were the iron core of the army, the hammer that would make the earth tremble.

At the end of June the army at last came down from the mountains to the town of Moukung in the far west of Szechwan, and here, for the first time since it had left Kiangsi, it joined forces with another army under the banner of the Communist Party—the Fourth Front Army under the command of Chang Kuo-t'ao, which had come from the Oyuwan soviet base in Hupeh.

Chang had fifty thousand men, well armed and rested, and under their shield the First Front Army could rest and recuperate. But not Mao or Chu Teh or Peng Teh-huai or Lin Piao; for them the meeting was a head-on conflict. Mao and his comrades had walked this far—four thousand miles—to fight the Japanese. Chang, however, had other ideas. For him the idea of establishing a soviet area in Shensi was mere wishful thinking. Instead, he argued that the two combined armies should march west into Sinkiang, where they would be outside the range of the Kuomintang armies and would also have a base on the Soviet border. Mao stubbornly opposed this idea. Still answering that deep instinct that told him that the place for the Red Armies was facing the Japanese, he held firm to his original plan.

In the previous struggle over the aims of the Communist Party at Tsunyi, Mao had, in the end, been able to turn to the army for support. But Chang too had an army at his back and one as loyal to him as the Central Red Army was to Mao. Mao was the Chairman of the Party, but Chang was unimpressed by this and held as firmly to his point of view as Mao did to his.

After fierce argument it was decided to move on to the town of Maoerhkai, both to rest for the next stage in the March and to discuss the matter further. But at Maoerhkai the decision was postponed once again; it was agreed to go on to Kansu and there make the final decision. This was agreed to by both Mao and Chang, and the army made ready for the next great obstacle to the March—the great Grasslands of Chinghai.

Looking back on the Long March—on the battle of the Hsiang River, the march through Kweichow, the race over the Yangtze gorges, and the crossing of the Golden Sand River, and the Tatu, and the passage of the Maanshan and then the Chiachin Mountains—it may seem hard to believe that the worst of the March was yet to come. But it was, and of all the experiences men went through in that year of endurance it was the Grasslands of which they spoke with horror.

The great Grasslands are really an enormous quagmire, hundreds of miles of oozing mud, covered with a carpet of coarse grass. Here and there nubs of higher land crop out of the bog, but otherwise there is nothing.

As the Red Armies moved out from Maoerhkai, the Grasslands stretched before them, empty and silent except for the sound of the wind in the reeds, the wailing of the marsh birds, and the sucking and bubbling of the swamp as it moved upon itself in its black depths. And the rains came, breeding a fog that wavered across the swamp, now thick, now thin, but always there, blotting out form and feature, so that the soldiers walked in a perpetual dusk. But even in this desolation people lived. On the hummocks was a tribe known as the Mantzu, a people as hostile as their environment. As the first column of troops moved uneasily out on the narrow twisting trails that snaked across the swamp, the Mantzu watched them through the fog, seeing but unseen, biding their time.

And now began the final winnowing of the Red Army. There was no food and no medicine. The water of the marshes was so bitter men could hardly drink it. The soldiers resistance to infection collapsed. They had boils and sores; every scratch turned septic and the acid water of the bog burned huge ulcers on their legs. Here men again began to die. Bodies claimed at last by exhaustion were dragged down into the swamp. At night as they huddled together in the never-ending rain, they were taken by the bitter cold into a sleep from which there was no awakening.

As the soldiers plunged deeper into the marsh, the Mantzu came from their dwellings to meet them. From the fog they flicked arrows, tipped with poison. Men felt a sting, and then a swelling, and then fever, and then nothing more in this world.

Leaving its dead unburied, the army moved on. In September the scouts came to dry land, walked for an hour, and another, and found the yellow sand of Shensi underneath their feet.

By mid-August the army was across the marsh and had re-formed. A general commanding a Kuomintang force in Shensi attacked the troops and was driven back with such fury that his army totally disappeared. A week later the Red soldiers were slashed at by the feared Muslim Cavalry who had guarded the north since the days of Genghis Khan, and it too was ground into the dust. Now, in October, the Red troops were nearing the end of their odyssey. They fought another fierce battle on the Liup'an Mountains as the wild geese flew south, and over the mountain, as snow fell on the bleak northern lands, they came to the town of Wuch'ichen and met cavalrymen mounted on stocky Manchurian ponies. The men wore red stars on their caps. The troopers of the Shensi

Soviet had come to meet them, and the Long March was over.

Mao himself shall have the last words: "Since P'an Ku divided heaven from earth, and the Three Sovereigns and the Five Emperors reigned, has there ever been in history a long march like ours?"

FOURTEEN

Of the ninety thousand men who had broken out of Kiangsi the year before, not more than twenty thousand made their way to Shensi. The losses had been appalling, although not all who failed to reach the new base had died. Many had been left behind to form guerrilla groups behind the Kuomintang lines; many had been left because they were sick or unable to endure the hardships; some few had deserted; but most of the missing lay silently in unmarked graves, five for every mile of the Long March.

Chang Kuo-t'ao did not appear to Shensi either, nor did Chu Teh. In one of the most astonishing events in that astonishing year, Chang, who had been leading his army in a column on the west of the Grasslands, had turned away from the rest of the army and marched into Tibet, taking Chu Teh with him.

Exactly why Chang did this, or why Chu went with him, has never been satisfactorily explained. Chu himself would never talk about it, and Chang's own explanation is somewhat obscure. However, the First Front Army, with Mao and Chou En-lai and Lin Piao, had endured together as a unity. The March had welded party and army together. Mao and Chou were in mastery of China, and from the ranks of those who marched with them came the commanders of the Chinese Army, which was Mao's rod to chastise those who opposed him.

But the Long March had taken its toll of the army and of Mao. The troops were worn out and suffering from disease. Mao, although he had not been wounded and had escaped serious illness, showed the exhaustion of unremitting fatigue and responsibility. Some of the Communist leaders wanted immediate action against the Japanese, but it was time to rest in the little town of Pao An, among the yellow hills of Shensi, and Mao knew it.

During the winter of 1935 and the spring of 1936, the Communists consolidated their base. The local population, the most backward in all China, was reassured of the army's good intentions. Delegates were sent to the wild Tartars and Muslims on the northwestern frontier. The troops who had once laid down their hoes for rifles now laid down their rifles for hoes and turned to the fields, for this was an army that fed itself. These were, however, relatively minor activities. After so long a time of making their own destiny, the Communists now waited for events.

During this time Mao's life was, as usual, extremely simple. His wife, Ho-Tzu-chen, who had been badly wounded by shrapnel but who had made the Long March, showing enormous courage, left Shensi for Moscow, where she was to have medical treatment, and Mao lived alone. His home was a cave scooped from the hillside. From this cave, with its simple wooden furniture, he looked out through a date orchard onto a shallow valley which held, in other caves, the foreign office, the war office, the headquarters of the Communist Party, a library, and a hospital.

In this valley Mao puttered about—reading, tending a small garden, where he grew tomatoes, and experimenting with plants from which he hope to make tobacco.

As it was for the rest of his comrades, this was a time of waiting for Mao, but his waiting was not idleness. As he slept and read and puttered about in his garden in the silence of the hills, he was working at the very deepest level of his mind. For Mao was not only a fearsome man of action, not just an astute politician who had learned his trade in the hardest school of all. His true strength, that which distinguished him from being a mere politician, was his imagination.

Imagination is not fantasy: it is the power to see that which is not there—but which will be. Just as a musician hears his music before the pipe is played, or the sculptor sees his statue before the stone is quarried, so the statesman sees possibilities in what is, as yet, the future, and in seeing them, helps to bring them to pass.

To see that future, to allow the imagination to work, requires time and silence, for it comes not from logic or reason—although they are both present—but from barely understood workings of the mind. And during that winter in Shensi it was silence and time Mao sought. For, beyond the relative tranquillity of the base, across the bare steppe-land of Shensi and Manchuria where the Japanese armies lay, the next stage in the enormous struggle of the Chinese people was maturing. Knowing this, Mao thought and slept and moved among his men, speaking of the vast war that was to come, and of the ever-present one, which the Communists never ceased to wage—the war for the minds of the Chinese people.

The struggle for the minds of the people was crucial for the Communists. For them every peasant was a potential revolutionary, every village a possible soviet base. Indeed, for Mao, the army and the party were not distinguishable from the peasantry. As he said at this time, "The deepest source of the immense power of war lies in the masses of the people. The army must be at one with the people and be regarded by the people as their own; then the army will be invincible throughout the world." Or, as he put it in a more famous phrase, "The people are the sea, and the army are the fish in the sea."

To this end the army was turned into a political machine. Wherever the Red soldiers went, the land was redistributed, rents were slashed, taxes remitted. Faithful to the principles worked out on Chingkangshan, the army behaved correctly. Nothing was stolen; everything used was paid for. Its soldiers worked in the fields with the peasants; its officers taught them how to read; its doctors gave them medical care. With this example before them, it was useless for the Kuomintang to talk of freedom and democracy to the peasants. To the laborer in the fields these were mere words. What he wanted was freedom from the rent roll and from hunger; democracy was his right to speak in the village without being beaten up by the landlords' bullies. It was these things that the Red Army brought to the villages, and it was this struggle for the minds of the people that the Communists were winning in Shensi in the winter of 1936.

At this state Mao was not thinking of a successful Communist revolution. The Communist Party was still too small and isolated for this. After all, and its forces comprised only a few thousand men locked away in the isolation of a remote province, a handful of members living dangerously in the big cities, a few guerrillas in the southern provinces, and the army of Chang Kuo-t'ao still wandering in the wilderness of Tibet.

But when, during the summer, Chang came home from Tibet followed by Ho Lung, the Red Army had a more formidable aspect. Now it numbered more than a hundred thousand men, toughed by war, dedicated, at one with their party, and all convinced by their leaders that the real enemy they now had to face was not the Kuomintang—it was the Japanese.

Indeed, it was clear to all that the Japanese were becoming more aggressive. The government of Japan was now under the control of the military, who, contemptuous of China and the Chinese, regarded both as raw material to be exploited for the greater glory of their warlike empire. Throughout the summer of 1936, Japanese troops in Manchuria were obviously preparing for trouble, and although Chiang Kai-shek spoke of the danger from within—from the Communists—many of his followers were more convinced of the menace of the Japanese. This was especially true of the Kuomintang armies facing the Communists. Most of these were from Manchuria, and, facing the Red Army, they were becoming convinced that it wanted to fight not them but the Japanese whom they could see strutting over what was their homeland.

Especially unconvinced that the Communists were the worst threat to China, and especially convinced that the Japanese were, was the Commander of the Chinese Manchurian armies, Chang Hsüeh-liang. Known as the "Young Marshal," Chang was the son of Chang Tso-lin, whom the Japanese had blown up in 1928. The Young Marshal had a mind of his own. When Chiang Kai-shek proposed a major attack on the Communists' base, he argued against it, and when in December Chiang flew to Sian, in South Shensi, to plan the attack, the Young Marshal arrested him.

The Young Marshal was driven to this staggering step by the fear that the attack Chiang was planning on the Communists would leave the door open for the Japanese to walk into

China. But not only did he arrest Chiang; he was also ready to try him before a "People's Court" and to use Communist judges. After he had arrested Chiang, he sent a plane to Shensi Soviet to fly the judges down.

On the face of it, this was a golden opportunity for Mao to dispose of his most formidable and dedicated foe. But Mao rose to his full stature. Overriding opposition inside his own party, he said that the Communists would not take part in the trial. Indeed, sending Chou En-lai down to Sian, he insisted that Chiang be released. Mao saw that, although Chiang was his enemy, he was also the commander-in-chief of forces beside which the Red Army was a drop in the ocean. Only the Kuomintang armies could muster the force that could stop the Japanese. Furthermore, there was also the danger that if Chiang was imprisoned or executed, control of the Kuomintang would swing to Chiang's second-in-command, Ho Ying-ch'in, who was openly pro-Japanese. Beyond these tactical considerations was Mao's bold recognition that Chiang, whatever his faults might be in the eyes of the Communists, was still the one man who could call on all China to resist the Japanese, and the survival of the Chinese nation was crucial to Mao's life.

For beyond the Marxist theory to which Mao had dedicated himself for twenty years, and beyond the struggle for political supremacy which he had waged since his youth, there was with Mao always the thought of China, with its past magnificence and present degradation. This was the center of Mao's passions, and the salvation of China was, for him, necessary for the salvation of the world. He made this clear in speaking to the American journalist Agnes Smedley in 1937. "The Communists," he said, ". . . are most passionately concerned with the fate of the Chinese nation and, moreover, with its fate throughout eternity. Only China's independence and liberation will make it possible for her to participate in the World Communist Movement."

Those were Mao's views, and there is no reason to doubt that he meant them. If the price of China's survival was the freedom of Chiang, then it was a price Mao was willing to pay. But he did not intend to let Chiang go free without forcing some concessions from him. The Communists wanted Chiang to agree to stop attacking them, to allow Communism to be legal inside China, and to form a united front against the Japanese. In return they were ready to stop confiscating land, to drop their provocative title of "Revolutionary Government of Shensi," and were, or said they were, ready to place the Red Army under Chiang's control—although whether either side believed in this last point is doubtful. When the agreement had been reached, there was at least the semblance of a united front with which the Chinese nation could face their aggressors.

In fact, the agreement of Sian is an astonishing event. Ten years previously Chiang had destroyed the old alliance between the Kuomintang and the Communists by his butchery in Shanghai. At that time it looked as if the Communist Party had ended its brief career in China; its leadership was demoralized, its followers dead, and Chiang the master of history. Now, against any conceivable forecast, the alliance was renewed and Communists had a say in the government of China. And it was Mao who had brought this to pass. As he had seen during the bloody days of the Long March, the call to fight the national enemy, the Japanese, had brought the Communists from the wings to the front of the stage. And now nothing was to move them from it.

The "Sian incident" closed with the Communists well pleased, Chiang chastened, and the Young Marshal perhaps regretting his patriotism, for Chiang had him arrested and kept him a prisoner for the rest of his days.

The affair had one other effect. Since the days of the Shanghai massacre, little had been known inside China of the Communist Party. Now, as news of the agreement spread, the Chinese began to wonder who were these men in Shensi who spoke so defiantly of the Japanese. Young men made the long trek north to see for themselves what was happening in Shensi, and their reports of the rigorous honesty of the Communist regime were compared with the corruption so manifest in the rest of China. The leaders of the Communist Party—Mao, Chu Teh, Chou En-lai—became names to consider, and their Marxist theories possible answers to China's problems.

Thus, by 1937 the Communist Party was being seen as a realistic alternative to the Kuomintang by many thoughtful Chinese, and Mao as a man worth considering as a future leader. But, in that summer, speculation was of less interest than reality, for in July, at the Marco Polo Bridge, the Japanese Army commenced the long-expected war.

FIFTEEN

The Japanese attack was brutal and effective. As Japan's Manchurian armies struck south from their base in Shanghai, troops poured out to seize the city and take control of the Yangtze River, thus threatening the heart of China. But, as in the earlier attack on Shanghai, Japan underestimated the power of Chinese patriotism. The years of humiliation, if not of defeat, were over. In both Nanking and Shanghai the Chinese troops fought with consummate bravery. Hammered by the big guns of the Japanese, slaughtered by their bombers, the Kuomintang soldiers showed that they were as brave as the Communist soldiers.

But bravery was not enough against the modern war machine of the Japanese. Shanghai fell after three months, and a month later, Nanking, the capital, was broken into and seized. In both cities the Japanese behaved atrociously. Nanking in particular was the scene of unspeakable atrocities deliberately designed to terrify the Chinese people into surrendering.

While the carnage to the south of them was under way, the Communists were true to their word and attacked the Japanese on their western flank. Under Lin Piao the Red Army took on the enemy in one major battle at Pinghsinkuan and gave a strong army the hiding of a lifetime. But at this stage of the war these were pinpricks. The main fighting was taking place in the Yangtze Valley, where Chiang was falling back on Hankow. Here again the Kuomintang troops showed what they were capable of under good leaders. At T'aierhchuang they outmarched, outthought, and outfought a Japanese army in a full-scale major battle. By the end of 1938, however, with the fall of Canton, Chiang had lost all the coast of China and, refusing peace terms, had retreated into the interior, founding a new capital at Chungking, two thousand miles up the Yangtze.

Faced with catastrophe, China pulled herself together. Although a handful of traitors went over to the Japanese and formed a puppet government, the majority of Chinese stood firmly behind Chiang Kai-shek. The universities moved west with the Kuomintang; whole hospitals followed them. Factories, newspapers, even the ragged armies of the warlords marched to join the fight. But Chiang had retreated into a vast trap. Locked away in the hills of western China, he was powerless to strike back at the invader, and his front line congealed into a defensive position.

In Shensi the Communists, although ringed by Japanese troops, were ready and capable of striking back. Long used to fighting against overwhelming numbers and superior armaments, they used their guerrilla tactics, slipping through the enemy's defenses, hitting at his lines of communication and depots, and then vanishing into the landscape. And while Chu Teh and Lin Piao were in the forefront of the battle, behind the lines Mao was thinking—and writing.

On the face of it, it might seem absurd for a man leading his people into a savage and merciless war to spend his time theorizing, but Mao was arming his men with weapons more important and more lethal than guns or bombs. Weapons need men to use them, and any man faced with the reality of Japanese bayonets might well ask himself why he should be there instead of seeking his own safety. The answer to those questions was what Mao was giving, and the fact that he had an answer is why the Communists and not the Kuomintang rule China now.

In 1939 and 1940 Mao wrote three works that were directed at his men's struggle. The first was the "Philosophy of the Revolution," which is really a restatement of the Marxist theory of knowledge. That is to say, it is an explanation of knowledge, of how we know things, of what our experience of the world is. The Marxists hold that there are different ways of knowing the world and that these different ways depend, in the end, on the social position of the person who knows. According to this, a capitalist will "know" freedom in a different way from a worker. A Marxist holds that a capitalist will "know" democracy as the freedom to exploit the worker, whereas the worker will "know" it to be the ending of this exploitation. Both will see the other's actions as a denial of "true" freedom, since their own freedom is restrained by the other's action.

However, true knowledge—and hence true freedom—is held by Marxists to lie in understanding the laws of human society and cooperating with them. In order to fly, men must not attempt to imitate birds, an action that would deny the laws of aerodynamics, but must learn those laws and make, not wings, but planes which use those laws. So men, to be really free, must understand the laws of society.

Of course, the Marxists make a claim greater than mere philosophic understanding. Marx himself said that he had not developed a theory but a method, a way of doing things. He claimed, in fact, that he had discovered the laws of society and that this discovery would enable men to make their own future. This is the inspiration Marxism holds out to its believers. They are marching with history, masters of the future, and as that future unfolds, by the understanding of its laws Marxists will make a new future for mankind.

This is what Mao said in his essay, but he spoke of China as he did so. "This process," he claimed, "this practice of changing the world, which is determined in accordance with scientific knowledge, has already reached a historic moment in the world, and in China a great moment unprecedented in human history, that is the moment for completely banishing darkness from the world and from China and for changing the world into a world of light such as never previously existed."

There is a real sense in which the truth of beliefs and theories does not matter as long as men believe them and the beliefs fill their hearts and spur them to action. Mao's troops were invincible because they believed that the future was theirs.

Mao thus told his troops why they would win, but in his essay "Protracted Warfare" he told them how they would win and what the cost would be. In this essay, the title of which could daunt the bravest heart, he summed up the experience of the Chinese Communist Party in fighting against gigantic odds. He spoke of guerilla warfare and mobile warfare, of the losses the army would suffer and the strength it would gain. The war against the Japanese would be a contest between a "dragon king" and a beggar—but the beggar would win, for he was one of untold millions. The war, he warned, could be of indefinite duration, but it would be won. In proclaiming this, Mao rose to a height denied most politicians. He spoke the truth, confident that his people would accept the truth, and in speaking of indefinite time, he guaranteed a definite victory.

Mao made one other important statement toward the end of 1939. In an essay called "New Democracy" he spoke of the political future he expected. He dismissed any thought of an immediate Communist state. True to his bargain with Chiang Kai-shek, he stated that leadership of China still belonged to the Kuomintang, but he was also careful to emphasize the increasingly important part that the Communist Party was playing in China's affairs. He could speak of this with authority and confidence, for he could point to the growing power of the Eighth Route Army and the war it alone of all the forces of China was waging against the Japanese.

Mao was also not displeased at the thought of a long-drawn-out struggle with the Japanese. Indeed, the longer the war went on, the more certain did a Communist victory over the Japanese and the Kuomintang become. As Mao very well knew, the Kuomintang had no answer to the plight of the peasantry, whereas he was confident that his own party had that answer. As the war dragged on, Communist influence, through the action of its armies and its guerrillas, could only spread, and with its diffusion would come victory in the struggle for the minds of the people.

Chiang Kai-shek, on the other hand, wanted a speedy end to the conflict. The sooner that came, the sooner he could settle his score with the Communists. But Chiang knew that, unaided, his chances of defeating the Japanese were remote. He needed allies, and for these he looked to the West, in particular to the Western democracies, those powers that had for so long been China's oppressors.

To understand this it is necessary to look again beyond China's borders and to remind ourselves that the history of the twentieth century can be understood only on a global scale, and that although, as Mao said, the center of gravity in

Chinese politics lay in the peasantry, the center of gravity in the world lay in Europe. And in Europe, as in Asia, the war drums had been rumbling for the past decade, and now the beat of the drums quickened as in September 1939, for the second time in twenty-one years, Europe marched to war.

Once again the combatants were Germany, France, and Britain, and their conflict sprang directly from the consequences of World War I. Of all the combatants in that war, the loser, Germany, had suffered the most grievously. Saddled with colossal payments to the victors, her economy, already weakened by the slump of 1929, had collapsed. Millions were unemployed and bankrupted, and her politicians seemed incapable of finding a solution to her problems. In despair the German people turned to the man who promised a solution: Adolf Hitler. And Hitler did provide solutions. Under his rule unemployment was reduced, the currency was stabilized, and a demoralized nation saw itself feared in Europe. Building up the German armed forces, Hitler invaded other countries. Germany grew rich and powerful as he had promised, but only because other countrues became poor and enslaved. It was a process that could not last. Hitler picked off the smaller countries of Europe one by one, but as his power grew, he came into conflict with the two other major countries, Britain and France. Both of these, shocked by the slaughter of the first war, had stood by, watching Germany's warlike rebirth, persuading themselves that Hitler would, in the end, prove reasonable and moderate. However, in September 1939, Hitler attacked Poland, a country Britain was allied to and whose borders she had guaranteed. Faithful to her treaty, Britain declared war on Germany, and Britain's ally, France, followed suit.

The implications of this for Chiang were obvious. Japan was Germany's ally, and he hoped that the Western democracies would assist him, the enemy of their enemy's ally. However, his hopes were dashed. Neither Britain nor France went to war with Japan, and in the west, Germany conquered France, seized Holland and Belgium, and signed a peace treaty with her only continental rival, the U.S.S.R. By 1940 Britain alone of the democracies was undefeated. Standing alone, Britain had no interest in the plight of China, and Chiang's hopes of Western help were crushed. Very much alone now, and fenced in by the Japanese ring of fire, the Kuomintang began to crack, and there were those in its ranks who saw the possibility of a patched-up peace with Japan.

Mao, of course, was aware of these developments and equally aware of the dangers to the Communist position if any sort of truce was patched up. He could also look at the growing strength of the Eighth Route Army, now numbering nearly half a million men, and the Fourth Route Army in south Anhwei across the Yangtze, which had some eighty thousand troops. Under these circumstances the Communist Party ordered Chu Teh to launch what was known as the Hundred Regiments Campaign, an all-out assault on the Japanese forces in the northwest of China. It was designed to make sure that the Japanese and the Kuomintang knew that the war was being fought on two fronts—and that the Communists had no intention of making peace. The offensive, which cost the Japanese twenty thousand men, had, as many Communist actions did, another purpose also, for wherever the Communist soldiers went they took with them their beliefs. Every raid into Japanese-held territory meant a spread of Communist influence, and by the end of the Hundred Regiments Campaign the Communists had guerrillas across the whole of north China, from Yenan to the Yellow Sea.

In 1940 Mao had every reason to be satisfied with the progress of the war. While Chiang remained bottled up in Chungking, Mao's forces were growing in strength and popular support. But 1941 was to change the picture. While the Eighth Route Army dominated the military scene in north China, the Fourth Route Army was beginning to dominate the Kuomintang forces in the Yangtze Valley. In December 1940 Chiang Kai-shek ordered the Fourth Route Army to move north of the Yangtze. This was strictly under the terms of an agreement already reached by Communists and the Kuomintang. The army, which had been engaged in some sporadic fighting with Kuomintang soldiers, nonetheless obeyed the order and began to cross the river. The front-line troops had crossed when, in January, the Kuomintang attacked the remaining troops, some ten thousand in all, and slaughtered them.

This action marked the beginning of the end of the alliance between the Kuomintang and the Communists. Although this was not clear at the time, it also marked the beginning of the end of the Kuomintang. From now on, no matter how vigorously Chiang Kai-shek might proclaim his patriotism, and no matter how defiantly he opposed the Japanese, the Chinese began to think of him and his party as those who, while fighting the invader with words, were ready to attack the only force in China that was battling the Japanese.

But although the Chinese Communist Party and its armies were gaining the admiration of the nation for their resolute struggle, Mao and his comrades now found themselves in a worsening military position. In 1941 Chiang Kai-shek imposed a virtual blockade on the north of China, and after a year of this the position of the Communists was serious. By the end of 1942 Mao admitted, "We were reduced almost to the state of having no clothes to wear, no oil to cook with, no paper, no vegetables, no footwear for the, soldiers and no winter bedding for the civilians."

In addition to this slow strangulation. in July 1941 the Japanese launched a bestial campaign against the Communist base. The name of this campaign was the Three Alls, which stood for "burn all, loot all, kill all." It is hard to believe that men could give such orders, or that other men could carry them out, but in that summer the Japanese did. Killing, burning, and looting, they created a desert across north and central China, leaving scenes of such horror that they cannot be described.

The aim of the Japanese was to make a wasteland around the Communist base and then, as Chiang Kai-shek had done in Kiangsi, encircle it with blockhouses and heavy artillery so that no living thing could cross the devastation. But although the Three Alls war cost the Eighth Route Army eighty thousand killed and wounded, and wiped out a third of the population of the Shensi base, the Communists fought back. They crossed the wastelands at night and roamed behind the Japanese lines, striking and stabbing in lightning raids. In the villages they found willing allies, for even those Chinese who had no cause to love the Communists supported them against the hated Japanese. The war was not only fought above the ground. Every village had a network of tunnels, often joined to the next village, and the Red soldiers moved underground, surfacing to strike again.

As the army waged this relentless war against the Japanese, in the base area the party was turning to the economic problems the blockade posed. A huge production campaign was launched to make the base self-sufficient, and Mao launched another campaign, one of equal importance in his eyes, although concerned with men's minds rather than their bodies.

Known as the Rectification Campaign, it was a vast process of educating the whole population of Shensi, soldiers and civilians alike, in the basic beliefs of the Communist Party. This teaching was necessary because the years since the arrival of the Communists in Shensi had seen a huge increase in their numbers and followers. Most of these recruits had only the vaguest notion of the aims of the Communists, and although they were ready and willing to fight, this was not sufficient for Mao. As always he was looking to the future, a future beyond victory—or defeat. For whatever history might bring, the Chinese people would remain, and the party and the army, if welded together by a common ideology, would lead the people to communism.

In the Rectification Campaign Mao was at pains to stress the importance of Chinese history and the Chinese Communist Party's experience. This was necessary because many of the Communists in Shensi still looked to the outside world for guidance. In particular they still looked to the U.S.S.R., the home of the first Communist revolution. But, clearly, by now Mao, while still paying lip service to the dominant role of the Soviets, and to Stalin in particular, was becoming disenchanted with them. He had grasped that the Chinese Communist Party had survived because of men like himself who drew their strength from their own country, and who based their judgments on their own, Chinese, experience.

Thus Mao, in his speeches during this time, was at pains to emphasize the validity of Chinese thought. In one speech he declared, "When many scholars of Marxism-Leninism speak, they can quote Marx, Engels, Lenin, and Stalin from memory, but they have forgotten about their own ancestors." And so, as the Shensi base was learning to live on its own material resources, Mao was teaching it to live on its own spiritual resources. This was the more important because in 1941 the Soviet Union, having been attacked by Germany, was fighting for its very existence as the German armies stood outside the gates of Moscow.

Locked in its own death struggle, the U.S.S.R. had little time to spare for the Chinese Communists. But as Europe, absorbed in her own affairs, turned away from China, another giant nation, the United States, was soon to become deeply involved.

SIXTEEN

The dreadful Three Alls campaign in the summer of 1941 was part of a vaster strategic plan by the Japanese military, for, not content with dominating China, they had decided to conquer the whole of Southeast Asia and the Pacific. Their reasoning was that the major imperial powers battling in Europe would not have the strength to resist a Japanese onslaught on their possessions in the Far East. Indeed, only Britain had any military capacity left in the whole huge area. Controlling the Pacific from her naval base in Hawaii was the last of the great nations of the world not at war—the United States.

The Japanese knew perfectly well that if they were to carry through their enormous plan, they would engage in war with America, and to forestall any action by the United States, on December 7, 1941, without a declaration of war, an air fleet flying from a carrier force struck at Pearl Harbor and destroyed the American Pacific fleet. At the same time as Japan struck at the United States, it also unleased its forces against the colonial possessions of the European countries and within months had seized practically the whole of Southeast Asia.

China had now become an important ally of Britain and the United States, and America in particular was to become increasingly involved in China's affairs. Of course, the United

States had had a considerable interest in China from the early days of the nineteenth century. American missionaries had been extremely active there, and many Chinese, Sun Yat-sen among them, had been influenced by the ideals of American democracy, the more so as the American presence in China had never been as brutally evident as that of the other great powers. Consequently there was a certain friendly attitude in China toward the United States, and, among Americans, a rather optimistic wish to see in the Kuomintang a party anxious to spread American ideals.

Now this rather distant though friendly attitude was to become much more intimate. Recognizing that China was pinning down large numbers of Japanese troops, both Britain and America were anxious to aid her, but the main burden of providing the aid fell on the United States with its enormous resources. Along a road cut by immense labor through the jungles and mountains of Burma, the United States sent arms and supplies in huge quantities, and advisers were flown across the Himalayas into Chungking.

The Communists, of course, wanted a share of the arms brought in, and through their representatives on the War Council pressed for them. But Chiang was adamant; none of the American supplies were to go to his enemies. The Americans themselves were not opposed to arming the Communists. In the urgency of war they were prepared to overlook the obvious difference in belief between themselves, the defenders of capitalism, and the Communists, its enemies. In fact, many Americans, journalists and writers, who traveled to Shensi were favorably impressed by what they saw, and compared the vigorous war policy of Mao with the lethargy of Chiang. For their part, the Communists were ready to be friendly with the Americans. Mao made a number of speeches in which he praised the American achievement and referred often to his hero of boyhood days, George Washington, and to the struggle of the American people against the England of George III.

But all the overtures of the Americans and the Communists were in vain: the Kuomintang blockade against the Soviet base remained in force. However, this was less important to the Communists in the years following 1941. Mao's call for a great production drive had been answered; the Communist armies were by now virtually independent of outside aid.

Not only were they independent; they were growing in numbers and strength and skill. While the Kuomintang troops rotted behind their lines, the Communist troops grew vigorous with battle. Chiang saw the danger in this, and in order to give *his* men beliefs that could match the Communists' ideas, in 1943 he published a book called *China's Destiny*. But Chiang spoke in vague terms of a future beyond the war. He called for selflessness and self-discipline but did not say how these were to be brought about, and he talked in grandiose terms of huge programs of industrial developments to make China mighty. There was, of course, nothing wrong in these statements, but in the utter corruption of the Kuomintang regime they were insufficient. Words such as "National Regeneration" meant little or nothing to the Chinese soldier, yawning beside his rusty machine gun on the edge of the war zone.

In contrast, where Chiang could only talk of self-discipline, the Communists could show it: a Communist general eating the same food as his men and wearing the same clothes demonstrated selflessness, and in any claim to be the guardians of Chinese independence, the Communists hardly needed to argue. It was so clearly they who were doing the fighting against the Japanese.

However, the Communists made no claims to be the true leaders of China. Still thinking in terms of decades, Mao affirmed that the Kuomintang, the heir to Sun Yat-sen, was the party that would govern China when the war was won. He looked forward to a coalition government of both Kuomintang and Communists, during which the rebuilding of China would take place. In this period all classes, even the capitalists, would be allowed to take part in the governing of China. The battle then would be one of ideas, and it would be up to each party to persuade the Chinese people which ideas were the ones they wanted. What would be imperative was the need for social reform and an end to the civil war.

During this period Mao and all his colleagues spoke in terms of a distant future. The war against the Japanese, they thought, might go on for many years. Chu Teh admitted that he could see no way to defeat the Japanese militarily and said plainly that a war of attrition, a steady wearing down of the Japanese, would not defeat them. But although the Communists could not see, either on the political or the military front, any prospect of victory in the future, they were confident of the ultimate triumph. They were, it must be remembered, Marxists, and had not Marx said that history belonged to the Communist Party? Ultimately they must win; ultimately the future was theirs, and this comforting thought gave them the confidence to pursue their long, grinding struggle.

Chu Teh, in his tough, realistic way, was quite correct in saying that the war being fought in China would not defeat the Japanese, but the battle was not being fought there only. The United States, after a period of bitter defeat in the Pacific, was hitting back at Japan. Under General MacArthur, American forces were leapfrogging their way across the islands of the Pacific, inflicting heavy losses on the Japanese. The British, too, having stopped the Japanese advance at the border of India, were fighting—and winning—a brutal war in the jungles of Burma. Indeed, the war as a whole had entered a decisive phase. In 1943 the U.S.S.R. had destroyed a huge German army at Stalingrad, and the British had halted the German thrust at the Suez Canal at the Battle of El Alamein. By 1944 it was clear that the alliance of the Soviet Union, Britain, and the United States was certain of victory.

In these circumstances the Western powers began to think about the future of the world after the war had ended. Although that future was cloudy enough, one thing was clear: it could not be a world like the pre-war. The war was, or was claimed to be, a fight for democracy and freedom. Urged to define this worthy aim more precisely, the leaders of the anti-fascist alliance—Roosevelt, Stalin, and Churchill—had made a series of bold pronouncements in which they said that victory would bring the world Four Freedoms: freedom from want, hunger and fear, and freedom of speech. The war, it was claimed, was one for a better world, where inequality would be abolished and the unity and harmony of mankind assured.

With these declared aims, which encouraged millions to sacrifice themselves, it was obviously necessary for the West to alter its attitude toward its colonial empires and, in particular, toward its major Asian ally, China. Accordingly, in 1943, Britain and America renounced their old, unequal treaties. The renegotiation of the treaties took place, of course, through the Kuomintang which the West regarded as the lawful government of China. The Communists were not opposed to this. They recognized that the Kuomintang, the party of Sun Yat-sen, had a powerful claim to represent China, but they were bitterly disappointed at the refusal of the Americans to lend them, as well as Chiang Kai-shek, arms, money, and medical supplies.

Following the signing of the new treaties, relations between the Communists and the Americans were actually extremely friendly. The Americans were anxious that all the anti-Japanese forces inside China should cooperate, and they tried to get Chiang and Mao to agree on a common strategy. Mao, although he had reason to feel bitter about Chiang, the more so as his last surviving brother, Mao Tse-t'an, had recently been executed by a Kuomintang general, was quite ready to cooperate, but Chiang was unyielding. He and he alone, he claimed, was the ruler of China. Any cooperation with the Communists could take place only if they accepted that and—the crucial point—if their armies were placed under his control. As the Communists were not ready to accept either of these claims, the negotiations broke down.

This placed the Americans in a dilemma: which party should receive their aid? For them there was only one an-swer—the Kuomintang and Chiang Kai-shek. But, given the real conditions inside China, aid for Chiang meant enmity to the Communists. Mao was quick to see this, and during 1944 his attitude toward the United States began to alter. Although he regarded the United States as an ally and attempted to draw a distinction between American "imperialists" and the American people, he recognized the possibility of conflict with the United States. Grimly he warned that the Commu-nists were ready to fight the Americans, saying that as his ar-mies had fought the Japanese with only a few rifles, so they were ready to take on American forces.

This somber note was the prelude to the troubled relations between China and the United States, which were to have ex-tremely serious consequences in the future, although for all parties in China that future was still incalculable, for standing before it was still Japan.

Although as 1945 dawned, Japan was being levered from her conquests overseas, the task of finally defeating her seemed a gigantic one. Her soldiers had been fighting with in-credible tenacity, and there was a widespread and well-founded fear that if her home islands were invaded the losses to the Allies would be appalling. Even when, in May, Germany surrendered and the Soviet Union entered the war against Japan, invading Manchuria in August, the prospect of a war of annihilation in the enemy's own country was daunting. But in August the West brought the science of the twentieth century to bear on Japan's medieval fanaticism. Two atom bombs destroyed the cities of Hiroshima and Nagasaki, and in a state of shock the Japanese government sued for peace.

In the Pacific the Japanese armies surrendered to the Americans and in Burma to the British. The question left was, to whom should the Japanese forces in China surrender? Chiang was in no doubt at all: the enemy must submit to his generals. In no circumstances were they to negotiate with the Communists, for that would imply that the Communists were members of the Chinese government. Mao, of course, had other ideas. He intended to take over Japanese arms and territory, thus staking out his claim to *be* a part of the government. Accordingly, as Chiang instructed the Japanese commander-in-chief to surrender only to his generals, Mao ordered *his* generals to demand the surrender of Japanese troops facing them. In addition, and more menacingly, he ordered Ho Lung to occupy north China, and Lin Piao was instructed to strike into Manchuria.

By now the Kuomintang and the Chinese Communist Party were facing each other in open hostility. The fragile semi-truce the war had brought had broken down, and the stage was set for a resumption of the endless, dragging civil war between the two parties. But the China of 1945 was not the China of 1935. The Communist Party was now a major force in Chinese life. Its leaders were known and admired by the intellectuals and its policies of land reform widely talked about among the peasants. Above all, the Red Army was in being.

Chiang was not insensitive to this changed position of the Communist Party. He also knew that no one in China wanted another war and that public opinion would swing against anyone who started it. Accordingly, in a last effort to come to some sort of agreement with the Communists, he wrote to Mao asking for a meeting where, face to face, the two leaders of China could thrash out their differences. Despite fears for his safety, Mao accepted the offer and in August 1945 flew from Yenan down to the Kuomintang stronghold of Chungking to meet the man with whom he had fought unceasingly for half a lifetime.

Mao was fifty-one years old in 1945. He was a little fatter than in the days of the Long March, but still tall and erect, still reserved in manner yet possessing the steadiness that had evoked trust from so many men. He was still, in fact, very much the man he had been, except that, in honor of the occasion, he wore a new suit and new shoes—although he walked in them with that old peasant's lounging stride. He kept, too, that sense of artistry that added such an unusual dimension to his character. On his trip to Chungking—the first he had ever made in a plane—he looked down on the immensity of his country and was entranced by its beauty. As he wrote in his most famous poem about it, "Snow":

> The mountains dance like silver snakes
> And the highlands charge like wax-hued elephants,
> Vying with heaven in stature.
> On a fine day, the land,
> Clad in white, adorned in red,
> Grows more enchanting.

The poem is one of Mao's best as well as most famous. The lines show in their exhilaration something of the feelings he felt as, master of vast armies and unchallenged ruler of his party, he flew to speak with the lord of the Kuomintang as an equal. The lines, with their reference to feminine beauty, might also show Mao's joy in his new wife. For, some time after the Long March, he had divorced the faithful and courageous Ho Tzu-chen, who was still in Moscow, and against the furious opposition of the Communist Party leadership, had married an actress, Chiang Ching, who was noted both for her beauty and for her radical zeal.

When Mao landed in Chungking, however, thoughts of landscape and wife alike were submerged by greater issues, for what was at stake was the future of China.

As befitted the occasion, the meeting of the two men was formal; no one seeing them would have guessed that they had been at each other's throat for twenty years. Chiang, immaculate as ever in his beautifully cut uniform and gleaming boots, treated Mao in public with the dignity a man in Mao's position deserved, but in private he was not so polite. Years before, at Sian, Chiang had angered Chou En-lai by treating him with arrogant contempt; now he angered Mao, too, with his contemptuous and dismissive manner.

But the personalities of the men were of little importance. Even if they had loved each other like brothers, they could not have arrived at a truly satisfactory agreement. For while Mao was quite ready to join a government headed by Chiang, he was prepared to do so only if he had real authority, and Chiang was ready to have Mao in government only if his opponent had no power. The very root of that power, of course, lay in the Red Army, and as long as that feared instrument of war stood ready at Mao's bidding, Chiang could not sleep easy, and there could be no peace in China. Mao, of course, had no intention of laying aside the rod of iron that twenty years of suffering had forged.

Three weeks of talks brought about a complicated agreement of sorts, including the calling of a Political Consultative Assembly to discuss the future of the nation. Nevertheless, when, in early October, Mao and Patrick Hurley, the American Ambassador, left Chungking, the all-important problem of the Red Army had still not been resolved. Nor, as both Mao and Chiang must have known in their hearts, was it ever likely to be except through force of arms. A lifetime of war had taught both of them that, in China at any rate, no truer words had ever been spoken than Mao's dictum: "Political power grows from the barrel of a gun."

Under these conditions of truce, or rather semi-truce, for there was continual skirmishing between the two sides, Mao returned to the new Communist headquarters in Yenan, in Shensi. Back to another cave, one still furnished with rickety wooden chairs. And there in Yenan Mao and the Central Committee to the Communist Party prepared for the savage struggle that was surely to come.

In his bastion of Chungking, Chiang, too, was making ready. Although the United States had sent its most respected soldier, General George C. Marshall, to try to find a workable compromise between the two sides, his efforts were in vain. And when, openly complaining of Chiang's stubbornness, General Marshall left Chungking, China, exhausted, ravaged, bleeding, staggered once more to war.

SEVENTEEN

The responsibility for starting China's third civil war in forty-five years lies on the shoulders of Chiang Kai-shek, but this is not to say that it was an act of personal malice or ambition. Neither he nor Mao nor any other sane man wanted China's agony to recommence, but beyond their personal feelings lay differing conceptions of China's future. Although the U.S.S.R., Britain, and America urged peace, both men knew that the only way the future of their country would in the end be resolved was through the ultimate judgment of war.

In China the mastery of war belonged to whoever ruled Manchuria. And in January 1946 the Communist army of Lin Piao was there. The vital importance of the area to China's security had long been known. From Manchuria had come the Manchus, who ruled China for so long; Manchuria menaced north China, which was defenseless against it, and if north China fell, so too did the south. This truth was doubly evident in 1946. Manchuria was now the powerhouse of the north. It had railways, ports, factories, mines; if the Communists gained a grip there, they would never be defeated. In view of this, it was imperative that Chiang move before his enemies grew strong there, and so, in the most fateful move in China's history, in July 1946, he sent his armies to war.

On the face of it, Chiang had reason to feel confident. Although the Communist Eighth and Fourth Route Armies could muster two million men, not all of them were trained regulars. At least a million of them were merely militiamen, armed with nothing heavier than rifles—when they had those. Against them Chiang could deploy more than five million men, all regulars and all well equipped by the Americans with the most modern arms.

Chiang's difficulty was that he had no direct link with the north, for although he controlled the cities, the countryside north of the Yellow River was in the hands of the Communists. His first task, therefore, was to win back control of the provinces of Anhwei, Kiangsu, and Shantung, through which ran the vital railways to Peking, Tientsin, and thence to Manchuria. His plans to achieve this were not lacking in boldness. Sending his best army by sea to Tsingtao, on the Shantung coast, he also attacked the Soviet base in Shensi. In addition, in order to split the Communist armies in Shantung, he blew the dikes of the Yellow River, diverting it to its old northern bed.

Had this huge plan succeeded, it would have been the end of the Communist armies. The Shensi forces would have been pushed into the wilderness of Mongolia; Lin Piao would have been bottled up in Manchuria, where he could be destroyed at leisure; and the few Communist troops south of the Yangtze picked off with ease. Then Chiang would indeed have been master of China, and with the promise of American aid in plenty, the Communist Party would have been doomed.

But Chiang had seriously underestimated the fighting quality of the Red Army and, more disastrously, had completely misjudged the caliber of the Communist High Command. For although his attack on Shensi appeared highly successful—the Communist "capital" of Shensi was captured—he failed to realize that Mao was quite content to have the Kuomintang army wandering about an area that had no value at all for Chiang. Indeed, Mao was quite happy to roam about Shensi—using the bewildering tactics of march and countermarch that had outwitted Chiang in Kwangsi province during the Long March—while Chiang's Shantung expedition was being cut to pieces at the battle of Mengliangku. While the Kuomintang army trudged hopelessly after the Red forces in Shensi in the west, and while in the east they fought for their lives, Mao saw the gap they had left in their center and sent

one of his armies through it to the Tapa Mountains on the
borders of Szechwan and Hupeh, where they threatened the
whole of the Yangtze Basin.

The futility and ineptitude of Chiang's strategy was now
exposed. His eastern and western armies were cut off from
each other, the whole of central China was menaced, and
his armies in Manchuria were no nearer relief than they had
been a year previously. By Christmas it was plain that Chiang's position was extremely serious. A year of all-out assault
had led only to the dispersion of his five million men, and although he still held the cities of the north, the Communists
ruled the countryside. Since all means of communication ran
through that territory, the cities were at the mercy of the
Communists. In fact, as Mao had prophesied long ago, the
world of the villages had surrounded the world of the cities—and the cities were indeed helpless.

In July 1948 the Communist Party called a conference in
south Shensi, for although victory seemed to be theirs, the
shape of that victory was still to be determined. Should the
Communist Party now strike down the Kuomintang, or
should it be content, having demonstrated its strength, to secure a coalition with the "left" Kuomintang? If, in the face
of the sweeping Communist victories of the past year, this
should seem strange, it is worth remembering that three-quar-
ters of China remained outside Communist influence and
that, large though the Communist Party now was, and strong
though its armies were, they represented only a small proportion of China's six hundred million inhabitants and were
drawn almost entirely from the peasant community. As yet
the middle class was hardly affected by the Communist Party,
and the big cities had been lost to it since 1928.

Whether the Communist Party could now rule the whole of
China was, therefore, by no means a closed question. Furthermore, another factor had been added to the complex sum,
for again the Soviets had entered the Chinese scene. For
Stalin, China was only one piece in a huge and deadly game
of international politics in which the U.S.S.R. and America
were the players. Following the end of World War II the alliance between the two countries had broken up, and now
they faced each other on the very brink of war. The Soviet
Union feared that a sweeping Communist victory in China
might provoke such a war, one which the Americans, armed

with the atom bomb, would be bound to win. On the other hand, if the Chinese Communists kept up a running guerrilla war against the Kuomintang, the aid America would be bound to give the Kuomintang would prove a permanent weakening factor for her.

This was Stalin's view, and there were those in the Chinese Communist Party ready to agree with it. The other point of view was that the Chinese Communists should not shrink from their victory for fear of what America might do, not for fear of a world war, or atom bombs either. The Chinese nation would survive both, and if the nation survived, so would the Chinese Communist Party.

The importance of this argument cannot be overestimated. It contains the two propositions that have ever since dominated Chinese thinking: one, that China will not be awed by military might, even if that might is backed by the technology of the West; the other, that China, Communist though it might be, is first and foremost independent, deciding its destiny on its own terms and not on those of any other country whatever. The Chinese Communist Party had truly come of age.

Disregarding the Soviets, in January 1949 Mao sent Lin Piao his orders. While the other Communist armies pinned down the Kuomintang troops south of Peking, he was to take Manchuria. By September the Kuomintang armies had been locked into the cities of Mukden, Ch'ang-ch'un, Harbin, and Chinchow. In September Lin was ordered to capture Chinchow, thus sealing the entrance to Manchuria.

While Lin trapped the enemy in the north, Mao launched his armies against the Kuomintang forces on the coastal plain south of Peking. In a series of battles around the key city of Suchow the Communist General Liu Po-ch'eng broke Chiang's Kiangsi armies and drove the remnants to the Yangtze. Now all that remained was the capture of the great cities of Manchuria and the ultimate prize, the imperial capital, Peking. Although Chiang himself flew to the north to take personal command of the battle, his action was futile. Their garrisons starving and dying of the cold, one by one the cities surrendered. In a last effort to save the garrison of Mukden—one hundred thousand men—Chiang, with American aid, landed troops on the Manchurian shore and ordered the Mukden soldiers to break out to them. And indeed they

did leave the city. The whole army wandered a few miles
down the railway line and then, watched in silence by Lin
Piao's colossal army, they laid down their weapons in the
snow.

Having dealt with the south and the north, Mao turned to
the east. The Kuomintang army in Shensi was broken by Hsu
Chou and the north bank of the Yangtze cleared. And now
the turn of Peking had come.

The task of taking the city was given to Lin Piao and his
Manchurian army, now marching south to the pass where the
Great Wall defends the north of China. Peking itself was defended by General Fu Tso-i who had known Lin when both
were students at the Whampoa Military Academy in the days
when Chiang Kai-shek had been the commander. Fu saw the
futility of further resistance and was ready to surrender the
city; he quietly made arrangements to withdraw to Mongolia.
Unfortunately the truce broke down. Lin thought that he was
being betrayed and advanced south in a typical lightning
march. Fu then withdrew into the ancient walled city and,
with seventy thousand men, prepared to face his foe.

The siege was carried out with the utmost discretion and
politeness and not without humor. Reluctant to break the ancient walls with artillery fire, the Communists called in a professor of archaeology to ask his advice on the least priceless
part of the walls. He decreed them all to be priceless! In the
end no damage was caused to any part of the city, for Fu
surrendered.

The magnitude of the Communist victory is hard to
measure, but they knew its value, and when they marched
through the city in a triumphal parade, they showed that they
knew it. Lin Piao, who had never lost a battle, took the salute
from men who, hardened by twenty years of continual warfare, marched past him with the invincible swing of victors.
When, armed with the rifles of the Japanese, and riding on
American trucks, towing American artillery, they paraded
through the foreign concessions—for ninety years the symbol
of their country's humiliation—a new stage in history had
truly been reached.

And now began the last act in the drama of the old China.
Mao, wishing for a legal transfer of power from the Kuomin-
tang to his party, offered terms to Li Tsung-jen, the Chinese
Vice-President, but Chiang, although nominally retired,

vetoed them. Accordingly, on April 3, 1949, Mao ordered his armies to cross the Yangtze and complete the conquest of China. It was here on the Yangtze opposite Nanking that the British sloop *Amethyst* came under fire from the Communist artillery. The *Amethyst* escaped, running a gauntlet of fire, but her departure also marked the end of an era, for she was the last foreign gunboat ever to sail in Chinese waters.

One by one, the bastions of the Kuomintang fell—Nanking, Wuhan, Shanghai, Canton, Changsha, Chungking—until by September the Chinese Communist Party and the Red Army ruled the whole of their vast country—from the frozen deserts of northern Manchuria to the tropical forests of Yunnan, and from the waters of the Yellow Sea to the mountains of Tibet, where, then and forever, the dead of the Long March lie.

In September 1949 the Central Committee of the Communist Party moved to Peking, and on October 1, Mao, with Chu Teh and Chou En-lai at his side, stood on the T'ien An Men square. Wearing a cloth cap and dressed as always in rough peasant clothes, coughing a little in the chill autumn wind, standing where the Emperor had stood, and looking over the city where once he had walked coatless—Mao stepped forward a little and, before an enormous crowd, declared the foundation of the People's Government of China. "We have stood up," he declared. "We will never be humiliated again. Let the earth tremble."

EIGHTEEN

And so the impossible had happened. Only twenty-eight years after Chen Tu-hsui had rowed about the lake of Chiahsing in the gentle summer rain with his eleven followers, the Communist Party ruled China and all its millions, and Mao was master of its destiny.

There can be no doubt that when Mao spoke from the balcony of the Gate of Heavenly Peace he spoke not only to but for the Chinese people, and that what he said in his message was the reason that he and not Chiang Kai-shek was now the leader of China.

For Mao addressed himself to the two main classes of Chinese society: the middle class and the peasants. To the middle class he said that Chinese humiliation was at an end; no longer were they to be treated as second-class beings in their own country. China was to be both independent and great, and the middle class—the teachers, lawyers, scholars, managers, even the small businessmen, all those who had come into closest contact with the West and who had felt the sting of its contempt the sharpest—responded to this statement with a fervor that took the world by surprise. For the past century this huge, inventive, artistic, and industrious nation, its peoples portrayed either as figures of low comedy or as viciously subhuman, had been the pawn of any country which chose to send a gunboat to its waters. For the peoples of the West, secure in their wealth and power, the bitterness the Chinese middle class felt about this was hard to understand, and in fact, was never understood. But Mao understood it.

Mao also had a message for the peasants. As the middle class was to be freed from humiliation, so they were to be freed from want. With that promise made, it was useless for the West to lament the passing of freedom from China, for if the word "freedom" is to have any real meaning, then it must mean that men have a choice in their lives. For more than sixty percent of the Chinese people—for the landless laborer in Szechwan or the rickshaw coolie coughing out his lungs in the Shanghai winter—no such choice existed. To these people the Communists did, in fact, bring the basic freedom—that without which all others are academic—freedom from want.

Whatever one's own view of communism might be, one has to admit that Mao honored both promises he made on the T'ien An Men. The gunboats sailed away, never to return, the foreigners who remained were reminded, sometimes sharply, of their new position, and the poor were fed. The Communists instituted a system of central control of the food store of China, and a strict rationing system. Because of this, every man, woman, and child in China had enough to eat—not much, but enough—and although some had less than they were used to, many had more. For the first time in China's history there was no starvation. In the famine of the late 1920s at least three million people died in northwest China, and in Honan in 1943 two million more had perished—and these are merely two examples. It has never happened since, and that is worth considering by those of us who have never known hunger.

There remained, however, another class in China, one not likely to greet the Communist victory with enthusiasm—the rich. These, the wealthy businessmen and the landlords, had never known want, and their wealth had insulated them from the humiliation of foreign condescension. To this class Mao's message was blunt: submit or die. And, indeed, many did die. In the wake of the Communist conquest people were killed who were innocent of anything except having been born into the class of the landlords. But in 1949 these killings were not part of the government's policy; they were, rather, the paying off of old scores, acts of personal vengeance by men who had reason to feel vengeful. Nothing like the massacres of

Shanghai and Hunan in 1928 took place, and there is no evidence that Mao himself, who had lost wife, sister, and brother by execution, took any personal revenge.

In any case, the Communists had little trouble within their country. Gangs of Kuomintang soldiers held out in the hills as Mao had done in Chingkangshan, but they were little more than a nuisance. On the whole, as 1949 drew to an end, the Communists could look upon a united China and feel that they had the support of most of its people.

But although Mao could look with some satisfaction at the internal state of China, its international relationships were more difficult. The Communists were inexperienced in foreign affairs. Chou En-lai, the new Foreign Minister, had lived in Europe, as had Chu Teh, the Commander in Chief of the Army (now known as the People's Liberation Army). But the Europe they had known was vastly different from the post-war Europe. Mao had never left China. Indeed, his picture of the world was drawn largely from books and was interpreted in terms of a Marxism which was often ludicrously at odds with what the outside world was really like. He thought, for instance, that the Western countries possessed a working class eager for the overthrow of the capitalist system and massively in support of the U.S.S.R. and China, whereas the overwhelming majority of the Western working class regarded both countries and their ideology with the utmost skepticism—when, indeed, they thought about them at all. Mao was totally incorrect in his conception of the Western working class, but he was not wrong in seeing hostility to China among the international community, and in particular in the United States, and this hostility was returned by the Chinese.

Naturally enough, the West was not happy to see China joining the Soviet camp, and such was the bitterness between the two sides that many in the West, particularly in America, could not bring themselves to believe that Mao had won his victory with the willing aid of the Chinese people. It could have come about, they thought, only as the result of a plot by the Soviets, although China, in fact, had received virtually no aid from the U.S.S.R. During all the years of struggle what they had received amounted only to moral support and bad advice. But despite this, the U.S.S.R. was the natural ally of China, and in order to foster the alliance, at the end of 1949, Mao flew to Moscow for talks.

Mao went to the Soviet Union the unchallenged leader of his country, a man of world stature, both a dedicated Communist and an ardent nationalist, a believer in the greatness of his country and the greatness of its people. He was, in fact, a man who could feel, and rightly, that he was fit to walk as an equal with any other man on earth. However, when he met the Soviet leaders—or, rather, the Soviet leader, Stalin—he found that far from being regarded as an equal he was regarded as under Soviet tutelage. Stalin saw the U.S.S.R. as the leader of the world revolution, and he held that the interests of all Communist parties must take second place to the interests of the homeland of the revolution—Russia.

All Communists were expected to accept this view, and most did. But Mao was no ordinary Communist. Almost single-handedly he had changed the thinking of the Chinese Communist Party, refusing to accept the theories of men brought up in an alien society and adapting the teaching of Marx to Chinese conditions with brilliant success. Stalin, on the other hand, had been almost completely wrong in the advice he had given the Chinese Communists and, indeed, it was through trying to follow his orders that they had been brought to the disasters of 1927.

Still, Mao was ready to recognize the leading role of the Soviet Union and of Stalin. The Soviet leader had a prestige among Communists hard to understand now, and his country was the oldest and strongest of the Communist countries. It was, too, the only industrialized country to which Mao could turn for help. But he was not prepared to be treated as an inferior or as the leader of an inferior nation. And so, although he left Moscow with many protestations of eternal friendship and promises of help, there was an undercurrent of resentment that was to burst out in a flood of anger in the years to come.

Back in Peking, Mao was free to turn his and his party's attention to the reorganization of China. There were two problems facing the Communists: the cities and their industries had to be revived and the ownership of the land reformed. In their approach to both of these the new government was moderate. It recognized that there were different classes inside China and that the country needed the aid of all of them. The government allowed the businessmen to continue running their industries, on condition that they cooperated fully with the new regime. In fact, many businessmen were more prosperous than before, for the government shielded them from ruinous competition from abroad. At the same time it was made clear that this was not a state of affairs that would go on forever. At some time in the future all businesses would come under the rule of the State.

In their land policy the government was equally moderate. The first Land Reform Act in 1950 took away from the very rich most of their land and redistributed it to the poor peasants, but most of the farmers were left owning their own land.

In both these measures the Communists showed themselves to be practical and sensible. The most urgent need for China was to recover from the terrible wars she had suffered for thirty years. As long as people worked together, the State was content to let them live their own lives. This, of course, was not the ultimate aim of the Communists. Sooner or later they would set out to alter the nation and the people, to shatter all the molds of thought in which Chinese life was cast, and to create instead a new people—although what that people might be none among them could say.

And so in the summer of 1950 the Chinese Communists had reason to be satisfied with themselves. China was now a unified country; the countryside was tranquil, the cities bustling, the people behind the government. To the north and west she had a powerful ally, guaranteeing the safety of her land border, and the conquest of Tibet, whatever the rest of the world might think, had given back to China her ancient borders. Only one irritant remained. On the island of Taiwan was Chiang Kai-shek, permanently challenging the legality of Mao's rule. The Peking government had plans for him, too.

As the government came to grips with its problems, to the east, where the long peninsula of Korea curves like a scimitar into the Yellow Sea, the cold war was about to become hot.

Astonishingly enough, the causes of the Korean War, a war that led to Americans and Chinese killing each other and soured relations between the two countries for the next twenty years, are still not fully understood. After the ending of World War II Korea, which had been occupied by the Japanese, was divided, the north coming under Soviet domination, and the south under American. Which side started the actual war is still debatable. What is certain is that when it did break out, the formidable troops of the north swept aside the southern armies and appeared to be capturing the whole country.

At this point the Americans intervened. The North Korean armies were pushed back north, across the old dividing line, and toward the Chinese border by General Douglas MacArthur's forces.

At this point it was certain that the Chinese would intervene. Indeed, Mao had repeatedly warned that a foreign army on the Yalu River, the border, would not be tolerated. These warnings had not been listened to, although it was obvious that China would not tolerate hostile forces threatening Manchuria, her main industrial base.

In those years of the cold war rational judgment was clouded. Just as some Communists believed that the United States was the stronghold of a huge plot against them, so some Americans thought the Communist world was about to take part in a vast crusade against them. MacArthur certainly believed this. He thought that the Communist world offensive had to be stopped, and he thought that Korea was as good a place as any to start. Accordingly, he took his troops to the Yalu—and Mao entered the war.

After ferocious fighting, in which Mao's son was killed and in which the Chinese showed the strength of their manpower and the Americans their superb technical skills, the war ground to a halt with the country divided just where it had been three blood-soaked years previously.

The Korean War was an event of huge importance in China's post-war history. It confirmed America's and China's worst fears of each other: the People's Republic of China was not recognized by the United Nations, America put her naval forces between China and Taiwan, thus maintaining Chiang in his exile, and it led to worldwide suspicion of China and her motives, which was not really justified.

If the Korean War cast a dark shadow on the outside world, inside China it cast a darker one. In any nation at war dissent is discouraged and, if the war is seen as vital to the nation's survival, suppressed altogether. This was the case in China. The Communist Party tightened its grip on the country, harrying and killing its opponents. These were the years when "thought reform" became a feature of Chinese life. Thought reform is an attempt to prove not merely that an opponent is wrong but that he is in a real sense a "sinner." The huge meetings at which wrongdoers were pilloried and abused were designed to make the transgressor not only think that he was wrong but actually *feel* that he was. Once this internal, psychological change had taken place, then the accused could be given a penance, usually work of the most menial kind, and then be "pardoned."

Through these thought-reform movements the Communist Party was in fact showing its true colors. In the end the Communists' claim was that everything belonged to the State, even the ideas in men's heads. But not everything the Communists were doing was as sinister as this. During the war Mao proclaimed a great Women's Emancipation Act, which for the first time in Chinese history gave women full civil rights—always a cause dear to Mao's heart. In two campaigns, known as "The Three Anti's" and "The Five Anti's," corruption, bribery, dishonesty of all kinds were attacked with such success that these evils, probably the worst from which a poor society can suffer, were virtually wiped out.

But the Korean War had seriously altered both the balance of life in China and the party that ruled it. The war had brought to power men whose strength lay in organization—bureaucrats and planners, men only too ready to draw up blueprints for society—and to squeeze people into the right shape to fit their plans. Under this steady oppression the intellectual life of China began to show a rapid decline. Without free debate there can be no creativity, and without experiment no progress. If the State lays down laws for scientific or artistic work, it necessarily prevents such work from being done, for the very essence of experiment is to find out what is new—and what is new cannot be legislated for.

It was in recognition of this that, in 1956, Mao made his famous statement of policy: "Let a hundred flowers bloom." In this, Mao asserted that ideas—the flowers—needed to be given freedom to blossom. There is no reason to believe that Mao was not sincere when he made this offer of freedom. He believed that in any free debate Marxism was bound to triumph, and he also believed that the people of China were, on the whole, satisfied with their government. By relaxing the party's iron grip, he clearly thought that there would be a debate inside the system but that no one would seriously challenge the system itself. There was certainly a personal element in Mao's decision to allow free debate. In his rough and ready way he seems to have thought that if there were arguments the best thing to do was to get them out in the open and to let them sort themselves out. It was a typically daring action, one that did not meet with the approval of all in the Communist Party. Many of its members thought it reckless and destructive, especially when the policy brought forth a flood of criticism not only of the Communist Party's methods but of Marxism itself.

The criticism shook both the Communist Party and Mao, but other events took place that disturbed them more. In October 1956 Nikita Khrushchev, the Soviets' new leader, made a "secret" speech to the Twentieth Congress of the Russian Communist Party in which he denounced Stalin as a bloodthirsty monster.

Stalin, of course, was dead when Khrushchev made this extraordinary speech—and had been for three years—but the speech shocked the Communists of the world. For more than thirty years Stalin had been the ruler of the Soviet Union and the leader of the world communist movement. Although millions had died because of his tyranny, and although he had been guilty of the most staggering misjudgments, no criticism of him had ever seeped from the vast prison house of the U.S.S.R. On the contrary, he had been deified in his own lifetime, hailed as all-wise, all-benevolent, and all-mighty.

Khrushchev was undoubtedly right in what he said in his speech, but there was one point he did not make. This was that Stalin had not been an accident but the inescapable consequence of one-party rule, the logical result of the rule of the Communist Party. The Chinese, however, were quick to see this conclusion and to realize that it could equally well be applied to their system, the more so since Mao was filling the same emotional role in China that Stalin had in the Soviet Union.

But the attack on Stalin was seen by Mao as more than a slight on himself. If what Khrushchev said was true, it raised grave questions about the very nature of Communism. How could such a tyranny have risen from what was, by its nature, supposed to be an extension of human freedom?

This question was made the more pressing by the events that followed Khrushchev's speech. A wave of unrest rippled across the Soviet Union's subject states in Eastern Europe, and one, Hungary, rose in revolt against the rule of the Communist Party within and the U.S.S.R. without. Only after weeks of bloody fighting, with Soviet tanks squealing through the streets of Budapest, was the rebellion suppressed.

The Hungarian revolt shocked the Communist world, but no part of it was more disturbed than China. At first Mao was absolutely in favor of the Soviet action. Seeing the world through Marxist spectacles and with no real idea of the conditions of European life, he believed that the uprising was a malevolent attempt by the capitalists to reimpose their rule on the working class. On reflection, however, it became clear that this was not an adequate explanation: whatever the motive behind the revolt, it was obvious that the Communist Party and the working class had become sharply divided in Hungary. But how could this be? According to Marxist thought, there could be no division between the two, for the party was the arm of the working class. And not only the events in Hungary made Mao uneasy. The result of the "Hundred Flowers" policy had shown that in China, too, the party and the people were by no means at one with each other.

In an attempt to answer these searching questions Mao wrote one of his most famous and significant essays, "On the Correct Handling of Contradictions Among the People." But before considering this essay, another aspect of Mao should be kept in mind, one that demonstrates that in the midst of great events and with the fate of a nation in his hands, he carried with him personal memories, griefs, and joys, and that behind the public mask was a private face.

Liu Chih-hsün, a comrade and friend of Mao's, was killed in 1933. Twenty-five years after his death, in 1958, Mao wrote a poem for Liu's widow, Li Shu-i. The poem, "The Immortals," uses, as do many of Mao's poems, ancient Chinese myths to speak of his feelings, and to relate those feelings to both China's past and future. Wu Kang, looking for immortality, was condemned to cut down a cassia tree on the moon, but with each blow of his ax the tree grows again. Ch'ang O also sought immortality and was condemned to be the lonely goddess of the moon, where she is eager to greet new souls. Yang, which means poplar tree, was the name of Mao's first wife who was brutally murdered in Changsha city by its governor. Liu means willow tree. The tiger is Chiang Kai-shek.

I lost my proud Poplar and you your Willow,
Poplar and Willow soar to the Ninth Heaven,

Wu Kang, asked what he can give,
Serves them a cassia brew.

Ch'ang O, the lonely moon goddess, spreads her ample
   sleeves
To dance for these loyal souls in infinite space.
Earth suddenly reports the tiger subdued,
Tears of joy pour forth, falling as mighty rain.

Obviously this poem is one of great beauty; the image of
the moon goddess opening her ample sleeves has extraordinary grace, but what is intriguing is Mao's relating of Yang
and Liu to immortality. Ch'ang O and Wu Kang have tried
to find personal immortality and are punished by loneliness,
but Yang and Liu, who died for a great cause, have found
true immortality, for they live in history.

Mao was a man noted for his realism, his ability to see a
situation as it really was rather than as he would wish it to
be, but this poem shows that his realism is not the material-
ism of the mere power seeker or money grabber. It is illumi-
ned by the light of the creative artist, and in his artistry,
which survived battle and hardship, he revealed an altogether
unexpected tenderness.

But if in "The Immortals" he showed his poetry, in the
"Correct Handling of Contradictions" he showed his sense of
reality at its best. Although he refused to admit that there
was a conflict of interest between the Communist Party and
the Chinese nation, he recognized that inside the State there
could be and were contradictions between what individuals,
or even social groups, might desire and what the State
desired. However, he drew a sharp distinction between what
he called "antagonistic" and "nonantagonistic" contradictions.
By "antagonistic" contradictions Mao had in mind the basic
conflict—as he saw it—between capitalism and socialism, and
by "nonantagonistic" the conflict between, say, the individual's desire for freedom and the need of the State to impose
discipline in the subject's interest.

This can perhaps be best exemplified by thinking of a soldier in an army. It is not in the interest of a soldier to be
killed, nor is it in the interest of his army to have him killed.
However, for the sake of the army—that is, for his own
sake—the soldier may be killed. But even though the interest

of the soldier and the army may conflict in this case, it is a "nonantagonistic" conflict, whereas the conflict between the army and its enemy is, of course, "antagonistic."

All societies have to face a conflict of interest between what the State desires and what individuals want. For instance, a man may wish to drive on one particular side of the road, but the State will override his wish and, in the interest of all the people, force him to drive on the side of the road it chooses.

This is a trivial example, but most societies in the West take for granted that there is no real conflict between its peoples and its government. On the whole, the only genuine "antagonistic" contradictions inside democracies are those between the State and the criminal—it is worth remembering, however, that Marxists would not accept this.

"Socialist" states, such as China, are not in this position. They are at war with elements inside themselves. The State decrees that there will be no private ownership of factories, but there is still a class inside the state which, until recently, owned the factories and which might well wish for their restoration. In dealing with this class the State will necessarily be forced into aggressive measures. Its aim, after all, is to extirpate it. If this should sound as if the "socialist" state were ready to be ruthless, that is what it is prepared to be. But all revolutions have been faced with the same task. The great landlords of France had their power broken after the French Revolution, and the Catholic nobility of England never recovered their strength after the English Civil War. Nor, for that matter, did the slave-owning grandees of the southern United States ever regain theirs.

On the whole, Mao was satisfied that there was no deep-rooted antagonism between the Chinese people and their government. There was, he thought, a "unity of interest" between them, and as long as this unity was recognized, free debate could and should take place. But such debates, he said, must always take place within a framework of order, which, of course, meant an acceptance of the Communist Party and its aims.

The trouble with this theory is that, although Mao was not wrong in believing that the Chinese people were behind his party in its struggle for national independence and in its battle against poverty and illiteracy, he was not necessarily correct in believing that his people were behind him in his plans for their future. For the aim of the Communist Party was not just to provide a higher standard of living but to transform the very nature of mankind.

This is not a concept of government acceptable in the West. In democratic societies the role of government is seen as ensuring that the rule of law is upheld, foreign aggression resisted, and the basic wants of the people supplied. Beyond this, government interference is not welcomed; what a person thinks and does is his own affair. Not since the seventeenth century have the governments of the West thought it their task to teach beliefs, nor would such teaching be wanted. This is not to say, however, that the West does not have beliefs, or that these beliefs have not come about through violence and bloodshed, too. The very basis of Western society—the belief in individual freedom—did not drop from heaven. It was hard fought for, and its defenders won because the society in which it grew developed in such a way that the ruling class of the past stood to benefit from it as well. Before revolution had taught them how to say it, "freedom" was not a word often on the lips of the French kings, nor the English ones either, for that matter.

Nor was it a word that had been much spoken by the Chinese Emperor. It is arguable that most Chinese were, in fact, freer than they had been in the past, but when a man has done his work, he likes to lie back a little and enjoy himself. And now, when the Communists had ensured that everybody had his rice bowl full, his transformation into a new and highly problematical human being was not the first priority in Chinese minds.

However, Mao had laid down the guidelines for future criticism of the government. Criticism within bounds was to be allowed, and if not "antagonistic," actually encouraged. This last point is important because not everyone in the Chinese Communist Party was prepared to be as tolerant as Mao. There were many in it who believed deeply in their own dogmas. For them the "Dictatorship of the Proletariat" meant just that. The party representing the workers would lay down the line, and the rest of the population would accept or else. To men such as these the sort of open-ended thinking Mao was ready to accept was intolerable. Thus, unseen by the outside world, to which the Communist Party presented a united front, deep rifts were developing.

NINETEEN

It was not only among the ranks of the Chinese that division was taking place. More obviously, and more dramatically, hostility was growing between the U.S.S.R. and China. The reason for this lay in the actions of Khrushchev. Following his condemnation of Stalin, he had embarked upon a policy of increased freedom inside the Soviet Union and improved relations with the West. Khrushchev, an exceptionally sharp observer, saw that the Cold War was ruining his country. To maintain herself in the arms race with America she was pouring enormous resources into the new weapons of war—the intercontinental rockets with their unholy atomic warheads. To try to halt this race Khrushchev declared that he was prepared to enter a new era of "peaceful coexistence."

This policy was hailed with relief by all the world except the Chinese, who regarded it as a blatant betrayal. How could their ally be on good terms with America when that country used its fleet to maintain Chiang Kai-shek on the Chinese island of Taiwan, and blocked the mainland government from taking its seat in the United Nations? Of course, Mao had always said that the Chinese would be ready to be at peace with any country ready to be at peace with them, but they saw a difference between not entering into war and fawning on their enemies.

The truth of the matter was that the Soviet Union and

China had grown apart because of the differences in the development of their two countries. The U.S.S.R. was a huge industrial society, vulnerable to the great rockets, and after forty years of suffering, its people needed the increase in the standard of living Khrushchev was trying to give them. But China saw this policy differently. She saw a rich society joining a rich nations' club from which she was excluded. In order for the Soviets to have washing machines and television sets, China was to take second place in their councils and be kept permanently out of the United Nations.

This was an intolerable blow to Chinese pride. China's own struggle against national humiliation won, was she now to be treated as an inferior in the international community? And at the whim of that upstart, Khrushchev? But more than hurt pride was at stake. China now began to see her position in the world in a different way. From the very birth of the Chinese Communist Party, the U.S.S.R. had been its ally. Often the advice the U.S.S.R. had given had been disastrously wrong, but she had been at its side, and Stalin, whatever his faults, could not be faulted on his enmity to the West—to China's enemies.

But if the Soviet Union was to change, China could, too. If her rich ally was to be lost, China would find new allies—her real allies—and she would find them among the poor nations of the world. Years before, Mao had seen the Chinese revolution as a struggle of the village against the city; now he saw the world revolution in the same way. The world of the village—Africa, India, South America, Southeast Asia—these would be China's allies, and as the Communist Party had led the peasants of China to freedom, so would she lead the peasants of the world to the same destiny.

Mao made this position clear to the Soviets at a conference of Communists in Moscow in 1957. There Mao was openly militant. "The East wind prevails over the West wind," he declared, meaning that the forces of the Socialists and Communists in the poor countries were overcoming what he described as the imperialists of the West. The imperialists, he said, were ready to use the threat of world war to frighten the Communists into retreating, but they should not be frightened by such threats. By all means take the enemy seriously, he declared, but despise him in the long term. He would be defeated by fighting a series of wars in country after country. In a famous phrase he declared that the imperialists were "paper tigers," fearsome to look at but impotent to harm.

This theory of Mao's became known as the theory of limited war: a sequence of revolutions that would finally break the power of imperialism. It is fair to say that Mao was not proposing to start these wars himself. His theory was that the people of the poor countries would themselves rise in revolt, as had the Chinese. However, he was not prepared to approve any policy that would lead to a deal whereby the Communists stood back and allowed the imperialists a free hand in fighting such wars in return for a guarantee of peace between the major powers.

Needless to say, this theory was not subscribed to by the Soviets. They knew the might of America, and they also knew the incredible destructive power of the atomic bomb. Any conflict, they thought, could lead to the involvement of the two great powers and make a world war, with the use of atom bombs, inevitable.

Mao, however, was unmoved by this prospect. In a spine-chilling speech he dismissed the atom bomb. It was, he said, a weapon of mass slaughter, but what of that? If it was used on China, half its people would survive and they would carry on the struggle against imperialism.

This belief of Mao's has long been the subject of speculation. To Western thinkers it seemed incredible that any rational man could hold such beliefs, yet Mao was a man who weighed his words, and it is worth considering what he said from his point of view. In fact, in speaking like this, Mao was drawing on his experience of half a lifetime of guerrilla warfare. In the Kiangsi base, and in the war against the Japanese, the Communists had faced fearsome odds. But although both Chiang Kai-shek and the Japanese had been equipped with modern weapons of war, they had been defeated. Certainly any reasonable man would have thought that the Communists were doomed to defeat in 1927, but, inspired by their belief, and perfectly ready to die for it, they had survived and won.

What, in fact, Mao was saying was that the result of any future war would be decided by men and not by technology, and his assessment has not proved incorrect. In Indo-China first France and then America fought the Communists for twenty years—and both were defeated. Indeed, in both cases, not only were their armies in the field defeated but the governments of the two countries were deeply shaken by the war. As Mao correctly saw, war in the twentieth century had become a test of political willpower. The people of the West seem no longer prepared to pay the cost in life which a struggle against the Communists of the East brings. Nor is the West's enormous technical superiority of any value. In Vietnam the Americans attempted to control the war from the air. But even under the shadows of the giant U.S. bombers the fighting went on until the despised "little men in black pajamas" finally forced an appalled America to withdraw her troops. Nor, it would seem, is the threat of nuclear war any deterrent—especially as the Chinese now have a hydrogen bomb of their own.

Mao's theories have wider application. The West, the world of the city, is dependent on the world of the village for its food and raw materials. If justice is not done in the world of the village, where people toil like beasts of burden and go to bed hungry, then they will turn to China for their inspiration. The world of the city will then no longer be able to exploit the defenseless, and its own people will go to bed hungry.

Such were Mao's views in 1958, and he was able to force them on an unwilling Soviet Union and make Khrushchev modify his policy of friendship with the West, at least for a time. Nevertheless, it was becoming clear that the alliance of the U.S.S.R. and China was coming under severe strain. In fact, the impossible was happening. Against all Marxist teaching, nationalism was becoming more important than the sacred cause of international socialism.

It was this feeling of growing isolation that led to a quickening of social change in China in 1958. The country, it must be remembered, was still a nation of peasants. Although an industrial base was being built in Manchuria, the majority of Chinese lived in villages, on the endless treadmill of sowing and reaping, each, though he might work as hard as he could, raising little more than enough to feed himself. To increase the production of those patient and determined hands, the government called for the establishment of People's Communes. The land was no longer to be a patchwork of individually owned plots but was to be worked in common, and the labor force was to labor together, all sharing in the ownership, the work, and the responsibility. By these means the government hoped that food production would be increased and labor released for the great task of industrialization, which was to take place under the Five Year Plan announced in that year.

All this, one might have thought, was quite enough for the nation to digest in one year, but Mao thought otherwise. In May he announced that the nation was to make a Great Leap Forward. This dramatic title referred to his belief that now, in 1958, China could jump forward to self-sufficiency by tapping the creative energies of her enormous population. The new communes would make their own machinery, and even the steel for those machines. Dams, canals, hospitals, schools—all these would come from the people and their efforts, and if technical experts were not available, somehow the people would acquire the knowledge themselves.

The Great Leap was a huge experiment in which all China was to be the laboratory, but behind the experiment was the pressing need to make China independent of the Soviet Union. The steel the communes made could also be used to make rifles, and the hoped-for increase in food production would free men to fight in China's armies. If China should find herself at war, an enemy would be unable to knock out her industrial base by bombing, for the bases would be every village in the land.

There were other reasons for the Great Leap. Now that the Communists ruled all China, there was, as Mao saw it, a danger that the intellectuals, the bureaucrats, and the "managers" would play a disproportionate role in making the new China. The Great Leap was to help correct this imbalance. By taking industry to the countryside Mao hoped to ensure that the peasantry, that "center of gravity of the revolution" of which he had spoken in 1926, would remain the center of gravity in the revolutionary China of the 1960s.

It is also possible to see in the Great Leap an interesting and very important aspect of Mao's own personality. In common with the rest of the Communist Party he wanted to build a new society in which a new and nobler type of man would be created. According to Marxist theory, there had to be various intermediate stages before this could happen. But the fact that the Communist Party was in power at all was due to Mao's belief in years past that the peasants could jump over a stage in history and take power without waiting for that "bourgeois" revolution orthodox Marxists had claimed to be a necessary prelude to socialism. Now, it seemed, Mao saw no reason for China to go through another waiting period before progressing to the "collective" social organization that would be the beginning of communism. Had not the willpower and dedication of the Chinese people worked miracles in the past? Let it work another one now! At one bound the mass activity of the peasants would bring about a new kind of society, one in which the old beliefs, the desire for personal possessions, the insistence on individuality, the family with its inward-looking values—all would wither away.

At first the Great Leap seemed to be an astonishing success. The new system of large-scale food production and small-scale industry brought glowing reports of vastly increased harvests and the production of millions of tons of steel. But as the year passed it became clear that the figures given were enthusiastic rather than accurate—if the Great Leap had jumped over anything it was statistical accuracy. The communes, forced upon a less than enthusiastic peasantry, had led to bad harvests and actual sabotage, and the steel the peasants produced was of such low quality it was of little use.

Not all the Great Leap was a failure. Millions of peasants received an invaluable crash course in industrial techniques, and many of the projects, such as dams and canals and wells, were highly successful. In carrying out these tasks a great deal was learned about the ability of ordinary people to improve their environment, and the work the peasants did helped to widen their horizons in the healthiest possible way.

But these were side issues. In its primary aim the Great Leap had failed, and, as it was so clearly identified as Mao's own policy, it was seen as a failure by him.

Mao undoubtedly felt this failure keenly, and, indeed, it was a serious blow both to his prestige and to his own most deeply felt beliefs. All his life Mao had faced the most colossal odds, but he and his comrades had overcome them by indomitable willpower. Now, it seemed, that will had failed. Instead of the Communists imposing themselves on history, history had imposed its intractable logic on them. In the face of this failure Mao did not stand for the presidency of the Chinese Republic in 1959. That post, although carrying more prestige than power, went to Liu Shao-ch'i.

The elevation of Liu meant a decided shift in power inside the Communist Party. Although ready enough to add his voice to the chorus of praise which, despite the failure of the Great Leap, greeted Mao's every movement, Liu was a man of a different type from Mao. He represented the more cautious, orderly, methodical thinking of the bureaucracy of the party, and under his influence it was likely that China's policies, both at home and abroad, would be less dramatic than before.

As Liu took up his office, and as the nation caught its breath after the upheavals of the year, Mao, as he had done in the past, returned to the Chinese countryside to consider his position. He returned to his native village of Shaoshan. While there he wrote a poem, and this, more than any speech or essay could do, tells us of the mood in which he walked about the village where, sixty years previously, he had fought his childish battles with his father, and worshiped the Buddha with his gentle mother.

Like a dim dream recalled, I curse the long-fled past—
My native soil two and thirty years gone by.
The red flag roused the serf, halberd in hand,
While the despot's black talons held his whip aloft.
Bitter sacrifice strenghtens bold resolve
Which dares to make sun and moon shine in new skies.
Happy, I see wave upon wave of paddy and beans,
And all around heroes homebound in the evening mist.

There is obviously a mood of nostalgia in this poem, a deeply felt sense of loss for the days when the issues were clear and the enemy obvious. The landlords raised their whips, and the peasants raised their bamboo spears against them. In those days, Mao said, men were inspired by great ideals; nothing was beyond them; they dared to make sun and moon shine in new skies. It is hard not to see in this memory of the past the feeling of a man who is faced with new, more complex, and more intractable problems. Still, the beans and rice wave in the wind. The land is fertile, and, although there is not the bloodstained drama of the past, new and different heroes have arisen: the peasants who stride home in the evening from their struggle to make the land give of its all.

However, Mao was not to be allowed to wander undisturbed among the orchards and rice fields of Shaoshan. In August, at Lushan, the Communist Party, of which Mao was still chairman, called a conference to discuss the state of the nation, and here Mao was faced with harsh criticism from a most unexpected quarter. Marshal Peng Teh-huai, one of China's great soldiers, a man with whom Mao had worked hand in glove for thirty years, and a man who had made the Long March and who was now Minister of Defense, voiced a violent criticism of Mao.

Peng's main criticism was that China was not yet ready to do without the Soviet Union's aid. As ready as anyone to believe that the "imperialists" were China's enemies, he nonetheless opposed the aggressive policy Mao was calling for. Also, he did not altogether agree with Mao's reliance on a guerrilla-type army. He wanted a modern, mechanized army with a clear and coherent chain of command, such as the West had, and the U.S.S.R., too. But hand in hand with this criticism went a deeper concern over the whole shape of the Chinese Revolution. Was it not time that order and method were brought into the national life? Had not the failure of the Great Leap shown that Mao's reliance on the will and on mass action organized from below—where it was organized at all—was destructive of the Revolution?

Peng was merely voicing the doubts of growing numbers of the higher-ranking members of the Communist Party, but at this time they had not the strength to do more than voice their doubts. Even that was a perilous thing to do, for although Mao's position had been weakened, he was still the major figure in the Chinese Communist Party. Accordingly, Peng found himself isolated and lost his post as Minister of Defense, which went, instead, to Lin Piao.

The dismissal of Peng might be thought strange in view of the undoubted failure of the Great Leap, but Mao was not to be faulted on the courage of his convictions. Although the attempt at a rapid industrialization had failed, and although China was still almost totally dependent on the Soviets for technical aid and advice, Mao maintained his bitter hostility toward Khrushchev and his policy. So sharp were Mao's words that in 1960 Khrushchev's anger finally exploded. In a speech in Romania he openly called the Chinese madmen and accused Mao of blind folly in thinking of using Chinese infantry against the weapons of the twentieth century.

With such acrid language being used, a final break in the alliance between the countries was inevitable, and in 1960 Khrushchev withdrew all Soviet experts from China, leaving huge dams unfinished, factories roofless, and students half trained. This was a damaging blow, since the chaos of the Great Leap was still manifest everywhere in the countryside, and in 1960 appalling weather ruined the harvest. The years 1960, 1961, and 1962 were years of the utmost hardship, even for a nation long used to distress. Only the most severe rationing, imposed with the utmost rigor, kept the country fed. That the country *was* fed shows the strength, honesty, and ability of the Communist Party. Seriously troubled though it might be by differences of opinion, it was still an able and unified body of dedicated men.

The near famine imposed more rational policies on China, and these policies meant that men had to be found who were able to implement them. This in turn meant that the shift in power that had begun with Liu Shao-ch'i's election to the presidency was now hastened. There is no doubt that the new men were of the highest ability. During the next few years China made truly remarkable progress. A whole generation of scientists, doctors, and technicians was trained, the all-important flood-control system was strengthened, vital heavy industrial and chemical plants were built, giving China her longed-for independence from the West's technology, and the living standard of the whole people was raised. Should this not seem such an extraordinary achievement, it is worthwhile comparing it with the progress of China's neighbor, India, during the same period. There, despite massive foreign aid denied to China, the basic problem of feeding the people was not dealt with and conditions of living for the great majority actually deteriorated.

During these years of steady improvement, Mao slipped into a kind of semi-retirement. Although he spoke on the great affairs of the nation, he was seen rarely. So little did he appear in public that there were rumors that he was dying, if not, in fact, dead. It has been suggested that this retirement of Mao's was a preparation of the Chinese people for the time when Mao actually would die. However, it seems more probable that Mao was merely biding his time, watching the affairs of the nation—watching, thinking, and judging.

And there was much to watch, especially in foreign affairs. As the row with the Soviets blazed on, China came face to face with India in a dispute over the border on the Himalayas. Since the coming to power of the Communists, China had been anxious to adjust its borders in accordance with the boundaries of the old Imperial Empire. With the exception of Tibet, which the Chinese had invaded, most of the border disputes had been settled sensibly and peacefully, but India was obdurate in refusing to retreat in the Himalayas. After repeated talks between Chou En-lai and the Indians had broken down, China finally, and after due warning, attacked on the border, and the crack Indian troops were humiliatingly defeated.

This dispute was another cause of friction between China and the U.S.S.R. Khrushchev, frightened that the dispute would spread and drag the world into a nuclear war, urged the Chinese to be patient—but at the same time provided the Indians with fighter planes.

Of far more importance than this were the events taking place in Indo-China. There, in Vietnam, the most merciless of all colonial wars was about to erupt again. Vietnam had already been a battleground for fifteen years as, led by Ho Chi Minh, a coalition of Communists and Nationalists had fought first the Japanese and then the French, who had seized the country in 1883. This protracted and terrible war had ended with a French withdrawal, negotiated by British Foreign Secretary Anthony Eden and Chou En-lai, in Geneva in 1954. At this conference a compromise had been patched up by which the country had been divided between north and south, after the pattern of Korea. The chief point of the agreement had been that nationwide elections would take place, but this agreement was not honored. As is usual in such cases, the blame for this was laid by each side on the other, although it now seems clear that if the elections had taken place then, the Vietcong, led by Ho Chi Minh, would have won an overwhelming victory. But as the elections were not held, it was not long before the two sides were looking at each other down the sights of their guns.

If the Vietnamese had been left alone, there is absolutely no doubt that the North would have quickly conquered the

South, but at this stage of the war America began her long, futile, and tragic intervention. Believing, by a tortuous and totally mistaken process of reasoning, that her own and the "free world's" security depended on halting what it believed to be Communist aggression, America, first under President Kennedy and then under President Johnson, became ever more deeply enmeshed in Vietnam. By 1966 the United States had half a million men in Vietnam, and her air force was sending down a never-ending rain of bombs, napalm, and defoliants until it appeared that the whole of Vietnam would become a wasteland and the North, in a famous phrase, "bombed into the Stone Age."

The Chinese, of course, were not indifferent to this, and although careful not to become directly involved, were aiding the North Vietnamese. The war was having significant effect on internal Chinese politics, for as America poured in its men, machinery, and money, Mao was becoming convinced that there was a serious danger that China would be the next country to be attacked. This was not mere paranoia on Mao's part. As he saw it, America was determined to root out communism from Asia—why should it stop in Vietnam? Indeed, it was impossible for America to draw a line south of the Chinese border. Short of America's undertaking a humiliating withdrawal—one it seemed unlikely she would undertake—she would be forced first to invade North Vietnam and then China. This being the case, China would then have to decide what sort of war she would wage against America.

For Mao the answer was clear. China could not hope to match American weaponry, but she could match her will to win. As in the struggle against the Kuomintang and then against the Japanese, China would use her inexhaustible manpower and her huge spaces to defeat the enemy. The war would be again a "protracted war," one in which the enemy would be lured into the sea of the people—and there drowned. Such a war would entail huge lossess and endless hardship, and it would need a body of men, a vast body, that would be possessed of the selflessness and dedication that had so marked the Communist armies of the past.

Such a body could only come from a society that was itself selfless and dedicated, and China was not yet that. Like all other countries, it was full of people who were happy enough to cooperate with the government, but for whom the prospect of an endless and merciless war had no attraction at all. What is more, many of these people were the experts who ran China's cities and factories and who taught in its universities. Many of these people, although not Communists themselves, were sympathetic to the government's aims, but they were still of the old order. How would they behave in a protracted war?

Most important of all, there was the Communist Party itself. Was this still the band of iron men of the past, or had power softened them? Had they, as they bent themselves at their task of rebuilding China, turned away from the mightier task of leading the world revolution? Above all, had their exercise of power made them rigid and inflexible, no longer capable of suppleness an endless guerrilla war would demand?

Mao, at any rate, had no doubts. China must be prepared for the coming struggle, and that preparation must be a return to the purity of the uncorrupted Communist Party, the party of the Revolution, the party of Yenan and the Long March.

Already Mao had taken steps toward this goal. With the close cooperation of Lin Piao he had called for a reorganization of the army. All visible signs of rank, all signs of office had been abolished. Officers and men had been urged to regard each other as equal comrades. Political training had been intensified, with great stress laid on the army's revolutionary role, a role that had been played down since the Communist victory of 1947. In 1966 Mao called on the nation to "learn from the army," and it was this army, this kind of primitive Communist state, linked together by close comradeship and calling in the end for the supreme sacrifice of its members, that Mao had in mind.

This was, however, merely the prelude to Mao's plans, for only twenty years after coming to power and with a China apparently settled on a course of national prosperity, Mao had in mind nothing less than the complete remolding of his nation. He was, in fact, ready to commence a second revolution: the Great Proletarian Cultural Revolution.

TWENTY

This second Chinese revolution began in a somewhat elliptical way. The Deputy Mayor of Peking, Wu Han, had written a play based on an old legend about the dismissal of a loyal servant by a Chinese emperor. The play was violently attacked by the *People's Daily*, the official paper of the Communist Party and hence under Mao's control. More ominously, this attack was followed by one in the army's newspaper, the *Liberation Daily*. In the months following, newspapers across China carried violent denunciations of Wu's play, often to the bewilderment of their readers, most of whom had never heard of Wu, let alone his play. Following this, there was sharp criticisms of the traditional arts by Mao's wife Chiang Ching, now an increasingly influential political figure.

This incident, obscure though it was, was the opening shot in a bitter battle between Mao and Liu Shao-ch'i, the President of the Republic. As we have seen, Liu took his office after the failure of the Great Leap Forward and represented the "moderate" men of the Communist Party. To these men Mao's thesis of the coming "protracted war" was by no means welcome. They inclined far more toward Khrushchev's theory of peaceful coexistence. In other words, while not relaxing their hostility to America or their deep suspicions of the capitalist West, they were ready to suspend hostilities and get on with their own affair, the building of a mighty China.

Wu Han was one of these men. A supporter of Liu Shao-ch'i, his play, although cast in the guise of a historical drama, was in actuality an attack on the dismissal of Marshal Peng—himself an opponent of Mao's aggressive thinking. And as Wu's play was a veiled attack on Mao and his supporter, Lin Piao, so the articles condemning his play were veiled attacks on Wu and *his* supporter, Liu Shao-ch'i.

This opening salvo fired, heavier artillery was brought into the firing line. In November Lo Jui-ching, the Chief of the General Staff of the People's Liberation Army, was dismissed from his post. Lo, too, was a follower of Liu Shao-ch'i, and his dismissal meant that Lin Piao had tightened his grip on the army. With Lo gone, Lin, free from opposition inside the army, increased his drive to turn it into a political force. The army was enlarged, and a huge campaign was launched to increase the numbers of Communist Party members in its ranks.

This shift of emphasis did not go unnoticed. There was growing concern inside China about the role the army was playing in Chinese life. More than one newspaper outside the control of Mao and Lin Piao voiced their alarm and, echoing Mao's words of 1938, asked, "Is the party ruling the gun, or the gun the party?"

To this, Lin had an answer. In 1964 he had made a collection of Mao's sayings and issued them to the army. Now, bound in red, the *Quotations from Chairman Mao*—or the Little Red Book as it was humorously called in the West—was in the hands of every soldier. Faced with the taunt that "the gun ruled the party," they raised the Red Book and silenced criticism, for Chairman Mao *was* the party, at least for the majority of Chinese. Indeed, for them he was hardly a man but a legend: the savior of China, the guide of the people, the strong arm between them and the whole hostile world that surrounded their country.

Mao may have been the incarnation of the revolution for those millions toiling in the fields and the factories, but to Liu Shao-ch'i, Wu Han, and many others in the Communist Party he was only one man among many. To be sure, he was recognized as the outstanding man; nobody would have denied that it was from Mao's astounding insight and imagination that the success of the Communists had derived. But this recognition was far from an acceptance of infallibility. The Communist Party had its dogmas but they were to be handed down from the body of the party, not from one man, no matter how great a genius he might be.

Accordingly, as Mao and Lin began to tighten their grip on the life of the nation, opposition began to grow. In the regions into which China was divided, there was, if not active resistance, at least a kind of passive neutrality toward the Cultural Revolution—for now it was becoming clear what Mao's aims were. He was not only concerned with purging the party and the army; his objective was to place every aspect of Chinese life under the control, not only of *the* party, but of *his* party, and the only test for membership of this party was total dedication to the revolution. For if China was to enter its grinding struggle with America, it must be led by men of right fiber rather than of the right intellect. "To be Red is better than being an expert" was a slogan much used during the Cultural Revolution, and it was much misunderstood in the West. In advanced industrial societies the expert—the man who knows how things work—has a neutral role. His job is to apply his skills, and this, as long as he is paid, he is usually willing to do without considering whether or not his work has political implications. But in a revolutionary situation this may well not be the case. Then, political dedication might be of more value to the nation than knowledge, for the expert may well—and without dishonor—find his loyalties divided.

An example of this might be seen in revolutionary France. There, when France found itself at war with the rest of Europe, it did not depend for the command of its armies on the trained generals and soldiers of the old royalist armies, although many of them were willing to serve the new republic. Instead, it produced its own generals—Ney and Masséna and Soult—ex butchers and bakers capable of learning their trade in the apprenticeship of war, and above all, loyal to their cause.

It is toward this state that Mao was moving in the Cultural Revolution. The survival of Communist China could be guaranteed not by experts, for at least compared to the United States, she had few, but by the nation in arms led by dedicated men. One of Mao's most celebrated remarks had been "Trust the people," and he has often been criticized in the West for not doing so. In a democracy the test for this trust is free elections held at regular intervals. In China, of course, no such elections take place, and it is assumed in democratic societies that because they do not Mao's words are mere hypocrisy. But in launching the Cultural Revolution Mao was expressing his trust in the people at the deepest level of being, for he was prepared to place the future of China's revolution back into the hands of those who had made it—the poor and the unlettered.

Of course, it was not to be expected that the intellectuals of China would regard the Cultural Revolution with the same sympathy as those making it. They, after all, were to be its victims. Thus it was in the universities that the first determined opposition to the Cultural Revolution developed, and in particular at the senior university of the country, Peking. The capital was a stronghold of the anti-Maoists in the party, and it was the determined resistance to the Cultural Revolution of the university staff and the Peking Communist Party that led to the formation of the Red Guards. Significantly, these were composed of young people, those who had known no other China and no other leader but Mao.

These young people responded eagerly to the call for the Cultural Revolution, the aims of which even now were not clear to most Chinese. Brandishing the Red Book and chanting their slogans of the "Four Olds"—the destruction of old ideas, old culture, old customs, and old habits—they took over the schools and universities. What they proposed to replace them with remained uncertain—except that it would be new.

As the Red Guards paraded the streets and painted their slogans on the walls of the city, a fierce argument raged between members of the party. Liu Shao-ch'i and Peng Chen, the Mayor of Peking and a high official in the Communist Party, fought for their political lives against Mao and his allies. If Liu had any illusions left about the aim of the Cultural Revolution, they were now dispelled, for the Central Committee propounded the uncompromising slogan, "Fire on the Headquarters Staff!" Of course, this was meant metaphorically—nobody wanted a bloodbath—but with Lin Piao's troops surrounding the city it was a distinct possibility, and Liu and Peng were dismissed from their posts.

However, what might have seemed the end of resistance to

the Revolution was merely the beginning, for neither the Red Guards nor the army were having matters their own way everywhere. In the provinces many army commanders were reluctant to back the Red Guards, and where the army stayed neutral the old guard of the party was ready to strike back at the new revolutionaries. And this was true not only of fairly remote areas where both troops and party leaders were only too ready to keep the status quo. In Nanking, for instance, one of the four major cities of China, the party leadership kept its nerve and, supported by the workers' unions, although paying lip service to the new policies, kept a firm hold over the city.

But in the end Mao and Lin Piao held all the trumps. Mao's prestige alone would possibly have been decisive in breaking the power of the old leadership; with the backing of Lin Piao's bayonets and with complete control of Peking, there was no possible force in China capable of withstanding it. One by one the provinces declared for the new policy. Where opposition was still vocal, Chou En-lai, ever the conciliator, calmed fears and urged, successfully, an end to resistance. By March 1967 the government, severely chastened and purged, was back in power, and the Great Cultural Proletarian Revolution was over.

Or so it seemed. The trouble was that the Red Guards, having tasted power, were as reluctant as their elders had been to relinquish it. They seemed quite prepared to carry on destroying the "Four Olds" until nothing was left in China but the Great Wall. There seems to be little doubt that the Red Guards became persecutors, carrying their revolutionary reforms beyond all reasonable bounds. Anyone not himself a Red Guard was an object of suspicion, and those guilty of nothing but admiring the art of the past were tormented by public abuse, beaten up, and even killed. The Red Guards even found grounds for suspicion in each other: rival groups developed and pitched battles took place between them.

Among the army, too, despite the lead given by Lin Piao, there was dissension. Army commanders, heroes of the Civil War and the Korean War, were not likely to take kindly to the abuse of young men and women with little experience of life. In the provinces troops handled the Red Guards roughly, and shooting was reported from many places.

Faced with this growing division in China, Chou En-lai

stepped in, bringing all his skills of compromise. Refusing to take sides, he brought the supporters of Liu and those of Mao to common ground. As Chou was at this task of compromise, Mao, too, joined in with calming speeches, and where they were not persuasive enough for the Red Guards, Lin was ready to drive the lesson home in a different manner. By the end of 1969 calm was being restored to China. The universities reopened, the children returned to school, the farmer to his fields, and the mechanic to his machines. The fever was over; the patient was purged and, if not fully recovered, at least convalescent. And China turned to face its uncertain future.

TWENTY ONE

The Great Proletarian Cultural Revolution had left China profoundly disturbed, and it was a task of the first importance to bring back stability and calm to its troubled people. Was the Communist Party, as it was now formed, capable of doing this? When the Ninth Congress of the Party was called in 1969, many observers were disturbed by the many military representatives present. Once again the specter of the gun ruling the party was raised, and it was a frightening spectacle to the civilians in the party. For, although party and army had been inseparable since the days of the Long March, the possibility of the army's taking over the party was never far from the minds of the civilian party members. Indeed, the fear of a military dictatorship had haunted all revolutionaries since the days when Napoleon had ridden to power on the back of the French Revolution. If such a figure was to arise in China, Lin Piao looked the part. Already head of the army, he was officially Mao's successor and had shown during the Cultural Revolution that he was ready to use his soldiers against his opponents. But even this was not the full extent of his reach for power. The Ninth Congress was preparing a draft for the new constitution of China, and one of its proposals was that a new post of Head of State should be established. If this was done, Lin would inherit the post and become master of the whole nation.

At this point Mao intervened. Seeing the danger of such a concentration of power in the hands of one man, he took steps to have the clause of Head of State struck from the draft constitution. There is evidence that Lin did not take kindly to this, seeing it as a sign that Mao was backing out of the close alliance of the past years. And if he did think this, he was not wrong. Mao had not launched the Cultural Revolution in order to see control of China handed over to one man. Indeed, at this time Mao was taking steps to curb the more extravagant praises offered to himself by the party.

Nor was Mao anxious to see Lin exercise too much influence on foreign policy. Although the Cultural Revolution had prepared China for a war, Mao was not looking for one. In fact, in the hands of the urbane and moderate Chou En-lai, Chinese foreign policy was becoming more conciliatory, especially toward the superpowers, the Soviet Union and the United States. From what is known, it is unlikely that Lin was in favor of this new policy. He was a fighting man and a revolutionary; war was his business and revolutionary war his life. So, as Chou patiently changed the face of Chinese diplomacy from a scowl to a smile, Lin, in his stronghold in Peking, grew increasingly remote from his allies, Mao and Chou.

But whether Lin agreed or not, Chou pursued his policy of détente. Following fighting between Chinese and Soviet soldiers at Chenpao Island in the Ussuri River in Manchuria, he started negotiations with the U.S.S.R.; for the first time in a decade the two nations spoke to each other in a civilized manner. Important though this was, it was nothing compared with the shift in attitude toward the other world power, America, for as the danger of war in the north receded, relations between America and China began to undergo a profound change.

Since the Communist victory in 1949, America had regarded China as a leper in the international community, and she had not forgotten that American soldiers had been killed by the Chinese in the Korean War. This loathing was returned by China who, with equal resentment, remembered that Chinese troops had been killed by Americans. But China had other, longer-lasting grievances. America operated a trade embargo against China, and America's allies were expected to observe it. This embargo had effectively cut off

China from the technical assistance she had so badly needed in the years after the Civil War, and the Chinese thought of it with bitterness. Above all, America supported Chiang Kai-shek, still living on the island of Taiwan. Her fleet protected him, and it was her influence that ensured that Chiang occupied China's seat in the United Nations.

The differences between China and America seemed irreconcilable, but in 1969 the situation began to change, and the catalyst was Vietnam. While the Great Leap Forward had struggled to get off the ground, and while the Cultural Revolution had convulsed China, in Vietnam the war between North and South had raged on and on until it seemed that only the death of every living being in the country would bring it to an end. The war had taken the lives of two million Vietnamese and had cost America dearly. Fifty thousand Americans had died in its jungles, two hundred thousand more had been wounded and mutilated, billions of dollars had been spent—and still the war went on.

Even America, mightiest of the nations of the earth, was finding the cost too high. In the United States an anti-war movement had been started that was dividing the nation. Riots and civil disturbances were destroying the roots of American unity and had already caused the retirement of one President, Lyndon Johnson. His successor, President Nixon, had as his first aim the ending of the war, but to do this he needed the good offices of North Vietnam's ally, China.

This perfectly sensible and rational policy presented President Nixon with huge problems. For twenty years the American people had been taught to regard China as an enemy, led by fanatics incapable of reasoning, intent only on world conquest. Now, somehow, Nixon had to change this attitude and show, as President Roosevelt had with the Soviets, that diplomatic relations with a communist country were not the beginning of the end of the world. The negotiations would have to begin in secret and be revealed to the American people slowly, step by step, to accustom them to the idea. Accordingly, Secretary of State Henry Kissinger began secret talks with the Vietnamese and Peking, and as progress was made, President Nixon began to show his hand. In 1970, as evidence of good faith, he ended the trade embargo, then revoked the prohibition on American citizens traveling to China. The Chinese responded with their famous invitation to the American table-tennis team to play in Peking, and soon Mao invited Nixon to visit China.

These friendly overtures were not the product of a conversion of either side to the doctrines of sweetness and light, but a recognition of the realities of power. President Nixon was desperate to extricate America from the Vietnamese morass, and the Chinese were only too ready to neutralize their most obvious enemy. In fact, Chinese policy was strictly in accordance with Mao's views on warfare, although translated into diplomatic terms. For Mao had said, long before, that in facing superior forces the correct tactics were to identify the major enemy, then the secondary one. Neutralize the secondary force and annihilate the major one. And although America was China's most obvious enemy, she was being neutralized in order that China might then deal with what she regarded as her worst enemy, the U.S.S.R.

But not everyone in the Chinese Communist Party agreed with the new policy, and it seems likely that Lin was one of them. With a warrior's ardor he was ready to wage war on both the U.S.S.R. and America, and with a fanatic's fervor he wished to see Chinese life controlled by the pure and dedicated People's Liberation Army.

The differences between the leadership needed to be resolved, and in August 1970 a conference was held at Lushan with this aim. Ostensibly, the conference was to discuss the new policies, both foreign and domestic, but behind that was the role of the army—and behind that was the succession to Mao, and everyone knew it.

Lin himself spoke at the conference. He made a speech extolling the genius of Mao, but this, although it might well have been expected to meet with the warm approval of the delegates, was received coldly. The new emphasis of the party since the Cultural Revolution had been on collective leadership and mass action. The creative genius of the nation lay in the people, not in any one man, and although, as a matter of form, Mao was considered the exception to this, Lin most certainly was not. In extolling "genius" he was regarded as paving the way for his own elevation to National Leader, and, what was more serious, he was considered to be opposing Mao's theories of the leading role of the Chinese working class.

Whether or not Lin himself was aware of the implications

of his attitude is not known for certain, but that is unimportant. What counted was that Mao certainly saw Lin's speech in this light and drew his own conclusions.

Considering the situation, it is difficult not to feel a certain sympathy for Lin. In the history of the Chinese Communist Party no one had ever challenged Mao and won. Ch'en Tu-hsiu, Li Li-san, Wang Ming, Chang Kuo-t'ao, Peng Teh-huai, Liu Shao-ch'i—his opponents had come and gone, defeated by Mao's unique mixture of political craft, farsighted genius, and indomitable will. And now it was Lin's turn, for after the Lushan Conference Mao set out to break the power of his "Close Comrade in Arms."

Mao, however, was walking a tightrope. Although he was revered by the people and supported by Chou and the "civilians," the "gun" still loomed over the party, and Lin's finger was on the trigger. Consequently, if Mao was to cut Lin down to size, he needed a gun of his own; he needed, in fact, to win the support of the army commanders under Lin, and this was a delicate business. Men who have tasted power find it difficult to renounce, as Yuan shih-k'ai had shown in the days of the Emperor. But Mao was equal to the task. Throughout the winter and spring of 1971 he toured the military districts, whittling away at Lin's support, cajoling and, where necessary, threatening. Although command lay in the hands of the generals, Mao was ready in the last resort to appeal to the junior officers and the rank and file, confident that they would support him.

Mao himself described the process by which he broke Lin's power. In a series of homely metaphors he said that first he "threw stones"—that is, compelled the generals of the army to stop supporting Lin, or, rather, Lin's supporter, Ch'en Po-ta, who was used as a stalking horse. Then he "mixed sand with soil," referring to the way he weakened Lin's command of the army by adding his own supporters to the Military Affairs Committee. Finally he "undermined the wall," perhaps the most crucial step of all, by which he referred to the dismissal of the soldiers Cheng and Wei, ardent supporters of Lin, from the absolute stronghold of Lin's power, the Peking Military Command.

Lin, of course, had seen the shadow of Mao fall across his path, but what could he do? Mao's process of demolishing his support was slow but as irreversible as a glacier, and as pulverizing. By summer it must have become quite clear to Lin that he was defeated. When Mao, sure of his position, began to hint that perhaps the army needed a "Rectification Campaign," Lin is reported as having shouted, "I know what that means—the old man's looking for a scapegoat!"

Lin was not prepared to be a sacrificial victim. In August 1971 he took a plane from Peking Airport, flew north, and there, over the bleakness of Mongolia, his plane crashed—or was shot down by Soviet or Chinese fighters—and falling with it went Lin Piao, Close Comrade in Arms of Chairman Mao, Marshal of the People's Liberation Army, hero of the Long March, victor of Korea—and one whose reach exceeded his grasp.

TWENTY TWO

And now the story has drawn to its close, but it has ended in riddles and enigmas, as does life itself. Did Lin Piao really die in Mongolia amid the wreckage of his plane? The Chinese say he did, but the Soviets, who found the wreckage, say that nobody of his age was among the dead. And did Lin really plan to kill Mao, fleeing only when his plot was discovered? Peking says so, but there is no way of testing the evidence. And what happened to those others who challenged Mao? Liu Shao-ch'i and Peng Tek-huai are probably dead, but we may never know when or how they died. But the Chinese Communists are not assassins. The emperor Pu Yi, the last of the Manchus, whom Yuan Shih-k'ai deposed in 1911, was alive and well in 1965, working on a history of his family. And others, such as Teng Hsiao-p'ing, were deposed, only to rise again—although none fell from so great a height as Lin Piao.

There is no mystery about Chou En-lai. He has died; the mandarin's son no longer brings the skills of the Heavenly and Harmonious Empire to the Chinese people, finding, as he always found in times of discord, a middle road down which they could march united.

And there is no mystery about Mao. He is dead, and his death ended eighty-two years of hardship, war, and unremitting responsibility. When his infant voice was first heard in

Shaoshan village, in the province of Hunan, in the Middle Kingdom, there were no radios or television, no automobiles, no planes, and no napalm or atom bombs; nothing fell from the skies but snow and rain. Not many men can remember such days, and it was the measure of Mao's immense life that he could.

Older than communism, older than capitalism, the Chinese nation survives. Its peoples, nine hundred million of them, still stoop at their labors in the field but now hear the tread of the future as it draws near to them, even to the remotest hamlet. And what shape that future will have when they see its face plainly will be Mao's doing.

What has Mao's struggle brought to the Chinese people, these brave, patient, courageous men and women, the silent majority of mankind? Famine has gone from their doors, and flood no longer drowns them by the millions, like so many unwanted kittens. Girl children are no longer killed at birth or sold into prostitution. The ravaging diseases—tuberculosis, smallpox, cholera, dysentery, leprosy, syphilis—are virtually gone from the country. There are no beggars, the cities are clean and the people honest to an extent unbelievable to those who know the depth of Asian poverty. None of this could have been done without the cooperation of the whole nation, and that it has all happened shows, to an extent many in the West are reluctant to accept, that the people do support the government.

What of the minds of the people? Have they, as some maintain, been turned into robots, "blue ants," their every thought controlled by their masters in Peking?

There is a grain of truth in this. The old China had a certain tolerance, which has now gone. As in medieval Europe, musicians once traveled the roads of the Heavenly Kingdom, and acrobats, magicians, actors, peddlers—all giving color and variety to life. A man like old Mao Shun-sheng could struggle to independence; men like his son could learn to read and write, could idle years away, create, experiment, and worship what gods they wished. But these freedoms were as fragile as the porcelain and lacquer with which China enchanted the world, although more precious. They were shattered when the West kicked down the door of the Kingdom. It is worth remembering that, although Mao had his secret police, Chiang Kai-shek had his, too, and the reform of men's thoughts was not on the list of its priorities.

Indeed, the old order was passing away before Mao was born, and merchants in the City of London had more to do with its passing than Karl Marx. Once the warships of the West had reached Canton, the Empire was doomed. There were only two questions worth asking: How soon would the Empire go? And who would inherit it?

Western democracy had its chance in China. Hung Hsiu-ch'uan, the Bible reader who led the Taiping Rebellion, turned to it for aid, as did Sun Yat-sen. If the West was truly democratic and truly concerned with the well-being of the Chinese people, why did it refuse them aid? Was it not, perhaps, because democracy, even then at the peak of its triumphs in politics, art, and science, was not for export? Was it because the West wished the East to remain in bondage forever, producing those materials on which the West battened and grew rich, and consuming those goods the West did not require for itself?

If this is the case, then it is meaningless for the West to lament the Communist triumph in China, for communism was born in Europe and her ships exported it. It is useless, too, for the West to deplore the "rule of the gun" in China—if indeed it is ruled by the gun—for it was the West that took the gun there.

The West's penetration and dominance of the East were the product of a certain set of historical accidents that gave rise to a superiority of industrial techniques; it could not last forever. When it was over, the West was bound to withdraw. All empires have crumbled, and the imperial sway of Europe and America was no exception. It is often said that the withdrawal of the West began when Britain handed over the government of their own country to the Indian nationalists in 1947, but this is not so. The West's dominion over the world ended when the first Asians cast their own iron in quantity—and the Japanese had done this by 1854. From that day the reassertion of the East was only a matter of time, and the flight of the Americans from Saigon merely dramatized the end.

Thus Mao was a child of his time, one of many—Nehru, Sukarno, Ho Chi Minh—who have rejected the West's claim to universal sovereignty and who have led the rebellion of the poor of the world—for that is what the Communist Revolution in Asia is. At the moment, that rebellion is convulsing antique lands, far away, but unless the West greets it with generosity, it may soon find it at its own gates. The world of the poor is the world of the village, and Mao has shown that in the end the world of the city—our world—depends on the village. Our food and our raw materials come from the villagers; we depend on them; they do not depend on us. Unless the West learns to recognize the aspirations of the village, the villagers may respond by ceasing to work for us. If they decide this, they now have an example before them: Mao's China.

There is another claim for Mao which, from the luxury of the West, we might make for him. He once said that the man carrying things on a pole over his shoulder was a disgrace to China. What he meant by this was that the man with the pole—the coolie—is less than a man: he is a beast of burden, cheaper than a horse and quicker than an ox. Mao's real lifework was to take the pole from that man's shoulder and allow him to stand upright. In doing this Mao not only helped his fellow countrymen; he helped the world. China's poverty was a burden that the world could not have afforded for long. To break that cycle of misery it was necessary to extend the vision, not of the merchants of Canton or the scholars of Peking, but of the multitudes who knew nothing but labor. After all, a man bent double cannot see far.

In allowing this to Mao we should remember that China is attempting something unique in history. There, for the first time, a peasant community is attempting to transform itself, from its own resources, into an advanced industrial society. No other nation has ever done this. The Soviet Union already had a strong industrial base when she had her revolution, and the only other comparable society, Japan, built her industries with the help of hundreds of millions of pounds loaned by the London Stock Exchange. China has had no help, and if she has made huge and grievous errors, it is not to be wondered at. Perhaps if the West had been more generous such errors would not have been made.

In fact, China has only one real resource: her people. Behind the Great Leap Forward and the Cultural Revolution is an attempt to bring the people into the new society, to release the creativity latent in them. At the moment the Chinese people are being taught to condemn Confucius, are being taught, in fact, to condemn subservience, respect for authority, traditional behavior, reliance on precedents—all those beliefs that molded the old society. Much that is valuable is being lost in this process, but it is not a diabolical plot to destroy the minds of the Chinese; it is, rightly or wrongly, an attempt to free them.

Something similar takes place in any society moving from a peasant-based economy to an industrial-based one. In England in the nineteenth century there was a wave of popular education which, with its emphasis on thrift and morality, was designed not to encourage learning, but to develop a responsible and reliable working class. Within that society, the nonconformist churches, with their largely working-class membership, involved men and women in debate which, although it took place within a narrow theological framework, did produce a people capable of making the new society work.

The Communes and Workers Brigades in China do just such a job. That the process in China is more violent than it was in England is more the result of the rawness and violence of China's past and her present lack of resources than any villainy on the part of her leaders.

This rawness is evident in the events that have taken place since Mao's death in September 1976. As we have seen, Mao had always been concerned that power in China should be held not by "experts" but rather by "the broad masses" (to use a Marxist term describing the peasants and industrial working class). It should be led, of course, by the Communist Party, which is—and we should not forget it—the only political party allowed in China.

The Great Proletarian Cultural Revolution had been launched to ensure this, and the "experts" had been defeated, but the defeat was temporary. Sooner or later the problem was bound to emerge again, for society cannot be run by enthusiasm alone; plans are necessary, as are experts to run them, and administrators—bureaucrats—to oversee them. This fact is bound to lead to the possibility, to say the least, of a rift between the governed and their governors.

It is to the credit of the Chinese Communist Party that it is aware of this danger and does try to do something about it. The policy of *Hsia-fang*, the enforced labor of intellectuals in farms and factories, although not popular, was a serious attempt to link all classes through shared experience. However, in the end the problem remains: How does one run a society in a truly democratic way? How does one prevent a polarization between the bureaucrat, rightly concerned with the orderly development of society, and the radical, whose aim is to ensure that power remains in the hands of ordinary people?

This problem is common to all societies. What makes it particular severe in China is the existence of a group of Communists dedicated to the continual remaking of society in order that a new, revolutionary man might appear, and quickly.

It was to deal with conflict of this kind that Mao had written his essay "On the Correct Handling of Contradictions Among the People." The question that China has had to answer since 1976 is whether the conflict is "antagonistic" or "nonantagonistic." In other words, can it be resolved peacefully or only through violence?

In the years since Mao wrote his essay, the problem has become more difficult. The very success of the Revolution has meant the development of vast new industries and the growth of an industrial working class which may well have different ambitions and priorities from the peasants. This has been the case on the railways, for instance. Their huge expansion has placed heavy burdens on the railwaymen, and this has led to industrial unrest. In fact, it is possible that the "Center of Gravity of the Revolution," which in the early days of the national struggle Mao had detected among the peasants, may be swinging, however slightly, to the new industrial working class.

If this is the case, it might be expected that the contradictions in Chinese society would become sharper and the struggle between rival groups fiercer, and this has happened, beginning with the death of Chou En-lai.

When Chou died, a new premier had to be found. Both the "radicals" and the "moderates" wanted the position to be occupied by their own nominee. In the end the post went to Teng Hsiao-p'ing, a man of the "middle" and an administrator of proven ability. The election of Teng was resented by the radicals, led by Madame Chiang Ching, Mao's wife. Chiang was not a popular woman. Many Communists had not forgotten that she had taken the place of Mao's previous wife, the brave and much loved Ho Tzu-chen, who had made the Long March. In addition, and more important, Chiang was passionately devoted to revolutionary extremism. She had been among the most fanatical of the proponents of the Cultural Revolution and had made many enemies. Chiang and her radical allies led an attack on Teng. Behind Chiang, of course, was her husband, Mao, or, rather, she claimed to have his support, for Mao, ill and aged, was becoming an increasingly shadowy figure. However, whatever Mao's own views were, Chiang was able to use his immense prestige to have Teng dismissed. Hua Kuo-feng was elected in his place.

Thus it seemed that the radicals had triumphed, but the dismissal of Teng led to widespread disturbance, most noticeably in Peking and Shanghai, where Chiang Ching believed herself to be strongest. This was shown most dramatically in Peking.

In January 1976 the deeply respected and much loved Chou En-lai had died. In April wreaths laid in his honor in T'ien An Men square were removed during the night, apparently on Chiang's orders. The next day great crowds gathered protesting against this, beating up militant pro-Chiang students and shouting praises for Chou and his moderate policies. Neither the police nor the regular troops intervened. It was clear that both the ordinary citizens and the army were against Chiang's policies of incessant and ruthless change. In other words, Chiang and her associates were isolated from the two most important elements in Chinese life.

As events showed, Hua Kuo-feng understood this perfectly well. Unfortunately for Chiang, he was by no means as radical as she had thought. He was certainly not prepared to plunge China into years of further turmoil, and he was increasingly exasperated by Chiang's interference with the orderly process of government. During the spring of 1976 he was plotting with the army generals to get rid of Chiang.

On September 9, 1976, Mao died. One month later Hua Kuo-feng sent his personal bodyguard to arrest Chiang and her associates, the so-called Gang of Four. Radicalism was defeated and moderation had triumphed. In August 1977 Chairman Hua declared at the Eleventh Party Congress, "The Cultural Revolution is over after eleven years." And at this time Teng Hsiao-p'ing reappeared, as a deputy prime minister.

That this is so can be seen from the events of the ensuing years. Radicals have been purged from the government and civil service, great stress is being laid on scientific expertise instead of revolutionary fervor, and the new party Constitution lays emphasis on discipline and order. The leadership has also emphasized its desire to expand trade and technological links with other countries.

It seems highly possible that the changes in Chinese economy, its move to an industrial base, will mean that the moderates will retain power. In fact China is now beginning to behave as most countries do: looking after her own interests, coming to terms with actualities of industrialization, and realizing that she cannot live forever in a state of isolation.

However, it does not do to exaggerate the stresses in Chinese life. The way in which the Chinese people responded to the disasters of the great earthquakes in Tungshan, which took place during the height of the plotting and intrigues, shows a resolute people ably led. And even the differences among the leadership, bitter though they were, have not been resolved by assassination. Indeed, in December 1976, with Chiang Ching under arrest and reviled by the press, Peking Radio, completely controlled by the Communist Party, broadcast an essay by Mao deploring murder—a clear indication that the government was not considering executing Madame Chiang.

The fact that the Chinese government is able to adopt such a policy may be considered proof of the confidence it feels in the people it leads. The parades, the posters, the savagery or argument are part of a vast political debate in which the party and the government do try to involve the whole of the population—a salutary lesson for other totalitarian states.

This involvement cannot be attempted with a people sunk in ignorance, disease, and poverty, but only among a population that has been levered, to however small a degree, from the pit of hopelessness.

And so, when Mao stands before the bar of Judgment, whether it is God who judges him or the generations of the future, his defense might well be that he tried to raise the burden of poverty, ignorance, and disease from the shoulders of his fellow men. The proof will be the China of the future.

For Mao was only a man, his life merely eighty years of China's three thousand. What will happen to China, what its future will be when the pole is taken from the coolie's back cannot be foretold. History is as improbable as the growth of

a tree from a seed. The future of a country, of the world, is
in the hands of millions of men scarcely aware of what they
are doing—men walking in darkness, seeking what they
barely know exists. Friedrich Engels once said that historical
change is the result of many men willing change, each
wanting a different thing, and the change being what none
had desired.

But it is true that from the millions men do arise around
whom history bends, as the light from remote stars is bent by
the gravitational field of greater stars. The greatest of these
men have moved as silently as the heavens; Jesus and Buddha
were two such, but close behind them come others who have
given history a definite shape and changed the lives of their
fellow men; Lincoln was one, Lenin another, and so, too, was
Mao Tse-tung.

Although the Chinese Communists are not monsters—it
took the West to produce Hitler—too much of this book has
been about violence, bloodshed, war and death, and the
struggle for power. But perhaps ugliness is inseparable from
great change; the crucifixion of Jesus Christ was not pretty,
and all nations have been born in blood.

Let the last word go to a Chinese poet, Wen I-to, himself
executed by the Kuomintang. Looking at his country in 1938
as the Japanese armies marched across it, Wen I-to said:

> Here is a ditch of hopeless dead water.
> This cannot be a place where beauty lies.
> Better let ugliness cultivate it,
> And see what kind of world comes of it.

Bibliography

Ch'en, Jerome. *Mao and the Chinese Revolution*. New York: Oxford University Press, 1965.
This is the best-documented of all books on Mao.

Devillers, Philippe. *Mao*. New York: Schocken Books, 1971.
A selection of the most significant of Mao's works, with a useful linking sketch of his life.

Fitzgerald, C. P. *The Birth of Communist China*. New York: Penguin Books, 1978.
An excellent review of Chinese history from the National Revolution to the 1960s.

Han Suyin. *China in the Year 2001*. Harmondsworth, England: Penguin Books, 1970.
An extremely sympathetic account of modern China.

Payne, Robert. *Portrait of a Revolutionary: Mao Tse-tung*. New York: Weybright & Talley, 1969.
A lively and dramatic picture of Mao's life by an American who was in Yenan after the Long March.

Schram, Stuart. *Mao Tse-tung*. Baltimore: Penguin Books, 1974.

Primarily a political biography. One of the best books on Mao.

Schram, Stuart, ed. *Chairman Mao Talks to the People.* New York: Pantheon Books, 1975.
A selection of Mao's speeches and letters from 1956 to 1971.

Schurmann, Franz, and Orville Schell, eds. *The China Reader.* New York: Random House, 1967, 3 vols.
An invaluable collection of documents and essays.

Snow, Edgar. *Red Star Over China.* 1st rev. and enlarged ed. New York: Grove Press, 1968.
The first book to be written about the Chinese Communists. This latest edition has valuable biographical notes.

Wilson, Dick. *The Long March. 1935. The Epic of Chinese Communism's Survival.* New York: The Viking Press, 1972.
A vigorous account of the Long March, with numerous eyewitness reports.

The poems by Mao in this book are taken from the translations in *Selected Works* published by the Foreign Languages Press, Peking, 1976.

Epilogue:

China and the United States after Mao

In 1784, one year after the United States gained its independence by revolution, the Empress of China, a 360-ton privateer, left Boston, Massachusetts, for Canton, the great trading city on the Pearl River in the province of Kwantung. Her cargo was furs, lead, textiles, pepper, and, surprisingly, ginseng.[1] She returned the following year with tea (hitherto a British monopoly), chinaware, and cassia, an herbal laxative. The voyage showed a profit of twenty-five percent.

Although the profit was excellent, it was not quite the

---

[1] Ginseng, current "in" drink for health-food buffs, has always been regarded in the East as the most precious of herbal medicines, and was an important component of the Empress's cargo. It was mainly grown in Manchuria and North Korea and also grew in North China, but it was becoming scarce by the nineteenth century. It also grows in North America, where it was discovered by the British East India Company. This type is inferior to the Asian variety, and it may have been because of this that the Empress of China did not make quite the profit hoped for.

treasure of Cathay that had been hoped for, and although the voyage was hailed as a triumph, a note of disappointed expectations mingled with the congratulations.

This ambivalent note was to characterize Chinese-American relations for the next one hundred and sixty years. Dreams of a fortune to be made in the China Trade vanished as the extent of Chinese poverty became known; hopes that a new China would be built on the model of the United States were deflated by the facts of China's historical development; and the passionate wish of generations of American missionaries that China would become a Christian nation was thwarted by the stubborn Chinese attachment to their gods and world view, whether these derived from Buddhism, Confucianism, Taoism, or Marxism. American goods, politics, and religion, were not, it seemed, for export to China.

But despite all vicissitudes, the hope has survived in the United States that somehow the vast country across the Pacific can be influenced for the better—that is, that it can become like America. The present détente has given fresh nourishment to that hope.

Certainly there is an American school of thought that sees the thirty years of bitterness since the Korean War as merely an unfortunate interlude in two hundred years of excellent Chinese-American relations. This view holds that the United States has exercised a restrained, indeed beneficial, influence in Chinese affairs. America, after all, took no part in the plunder of the Chinese empire. Unlike the imperialist powers, she never enforced unjust and unequal treaties on China. Her Secretaries of State, from John Hay in Theodore Roosevelt's administration to Dean Acheson in Harry Truman's, have defended China's right to territorial integrity. American missionaries, aided by America's partial return of the indemnities for the Taiping and Boxer rebellions, opened excellent schools and colleges in China. During World War II, America aided China with men, materials, and money, and did its best to bring about a coalition between the Nationalists and the Communists. She did not interfere in Chinese affairs after the Communist Victory and was only reluctantly compelled to do so by wanton Chinese aggression in the Korean War.

This is one optimistic view. Through Chinese eyes (that is through Mao's eyes and those of the present Chinese leadership), the picture looks rather different. America, a Chinese might say, behaved in fact, if not in theory, exactly as the other imperialist powers did, merely sheltering behind the guns of the British fleet to do so. Whatever gains were wrested from suffering China America shared in. She stood aside when Russia and Japan tore chunks of her territory from her, and her protests were mere hypocrisy designed to ensure that American "rights" and interests were not damaged. America has always had a racist attitude toward China and treated Chinese immigrant labor barbarously. American influence prevented China from taking her rightful seat in the United Nations, and the trade embargo she enforced after the Korean War damaged China grievously. United States attacks on Vietnam and Cambodia were direct threats to China, and worst of all, America used her might to prevent the People's Republic of China from exercising her rightful authority over an integral part of her territory—Taiwan.

Furthermore, and both sides would agree on this, since the Chinese Communist Party took power in 1949 Chinese-American relations have been disastrous. After the Communists took power, America adopted a neutral policy toward the new government, even declaring that she would take no steps to prevent the Communists from entering Taiwan, where Chiang Kai-shek had taken refuge. However, the Korean War changed this policy. General MacArthur's lunge to the Yalu River in particular confirmed China in its belief that the United States was intent on invading her, while the subsequent full-scale intervention by the Chinese confirmed American fears that China was part of a vast, monolithic communist bloc intent on conquering the world by force. This was particularly unfortunate since Mao, then very much the man in command, had a reluctant admiration for the United States.

A wave of anti-communist and anti-Chinese hysteria swept the United States. The collapse of morale among American prisoners of war in Korea led to accusations of brainwashing and confirmed many Americans in their view that the Chinese were subhuman monsters. Senator Joseph McCarthy's witch hunt led to the hounding from office of the China experts in government, thus depriving the United States of their knowledge just at the time when it was needed most.

Under the influence of John Foster Dulles, President Eisenhower's Secretary of State, anticommunism became a crusade. The United States' Seventh Fleet defended Taiwan, with whom the United States signed a defense treaty in 1954. As previously mentioned, American influence helped to keep the People's Republic of China from taking her seat in the United Nations, and the trade embargo of China, enforced on the rest of the Western world by the United States, seriously damaged China's progress. So deeply rooted was this anti-Chinese attitude that at the Geneva Conference, which was convened in 1954 to end the French-Vietnamese war, Dulles refused to shake hands with Chou En-lai. Although the United States Government did not oppose the settlement, it refused to sign the Accord, thus opening the way for the disastrous American intervention in Vietnam.

Furthermore, the United States built a series of military alliances against China in the Pacific, SEATO (SouthEast Asia Treaty Organization), and ANZUS (Australia-New Zealand-United States), and these could only be regarded by the Chinese as direct threats to them. In return, the Chinese could mount only a futile propaganda barrage, the language of which probably did more harm to the Chinese in the eyes of the world than it did to the United States.

However, in 1954, when Chinese-American relations were at rock bottom, Chou En-lai made an open offer at the Bandung Conference of Asian and African States to sit down with the United States and negotiate outstanding differences. Although this led to the opening of semi-secret talks in Europe, and although these talks continued for years, little came of them.

For the next sixteen years, shifts in the relations between the two countries were glacial. Public opinion in the United States was against any détente, and the Vietnam War virtually ended hopes for it. However, as we have seen, the need for the United States to extricate herself from Vietnam led to her taking a more realistic attitude toward China. Furthermore, shifts in opinion inside the United Nations made it clear that China would not be denied her seat for much longer. This clearly forced a different approach on the United States. In addition, the open rift between China and the U.S.S.R. helped to bring about a more rational view toward any possible Communist menace to the world.

Still, there are clearly other factors that account for the speedy and gushing rapprochement between the United States and the People's Republic. It does not call for any great wisdom to see that the most important of these is the other Communist giant, the U.S.S.R. Contrary to expectations, Mao's death did not heal the breach between Peking and Moscow. Any doubts about this may be resolved by reading the joint communiqué issued by the United States and China on December 5th, 1978. Apart from the historic announcement that the United States recognized the Peking government as the sole legal government of China, the agreement to exchange ambassadors and the tacit acceptance by the United States that Taiwan will eventually come under the rule of the People's Republic, the communiqué makes other statements about the maintaining of peace, both in Asia and the world. These aspirations are unobjectional and noncontroversial, except for Article Three. This needs quoting in full: "Neither (that is the United States and the People's Republic) should seek hegemony in the Asia-Pacific region or in any other region of the world and each is opposed to efforts by any other country or groups of countries to establish such hegemony."

Quite right, one might say, except that in the cryptic language of Chinese polemics "hegemony" does not just mean domination, or even domination by, say, Japan or France, but specifically, domination by the U.S.S.R. In other words (and one must assume that the diplomats were aware of this), the article is implicitly a declaration of a United States-People's Republic pact against the U.S.S.R. This is not, of course, a declaration of war, or even a sign that the United States is feeling particularly bellicose toward the U.S.S.R. However, there can be no doubt that it is the present state of American-Russian relations which have speeded up the Chinese-American détente. To understand the latter we must look closely at the former.

America's relations with the U.S.S.R. have been just as contorted as they have been with China. Following the breakup of the World War II alliance, the fear grew in the West that the U.S.S.R. was in a position to wage a victorious war against the Western alliance. In response to these fears, the American diplomat, and former ambassador to the U.S.S.R., George Kennan (himself a supporter of détente with the U.S.S.R., at a time when it was not popular to be one) propounded a policy of "containment" of the U.S.S.R.

Briefly, this policy aimed to pin down the bulk of Soviet forces in Eastern Europe while denying Russia access to world resources and finance, thus keeping her in a state of permanent inferiority vis-a-vis the West. This policy was adopted by the United States government and presumably worked to its satisfaction. Certainly it worked as far as the U.S.S.R. was concerned. For as we have seen, in the early 1950s, Nikita Khrushchev announced his policy of peaceful coexistence, which in turn led to a "honeymoon" between the United States and the U.S.S.R. Cordiality replaced frigidity, with the Strategic Arms Limitation Treaty (SALT I) as the policy's most precious offspring.

However, the past decade has seen a significant increase in Soviet strength, *not* in her rocketry, but most notably in the expansion of her armed and mercantile fleets. Although suggestions that this poses a serious threat to the trade routes of the world may be dismissed, the U.S.S.R.'s new deep-water capability enables her to exercise her influence effectively wherever she wishes, as in Cuba and Africa, in the same way that the United States fleets enable *her* to intervene wherever she wishes to do so, as in Vietnam, the Dominican Republic, and Lebanon, to take a few examples.

The morality of this need not concern us here. But to Washington, the new U.S.S.R. capacity is an alarming development. The struggle for the Third World appears on the way to being lost as, with Soviet support, country after country, from Algeria to Zimbabwe, declares itself a "socialist" state.

With this in mind, it is not unreasonable to suggest that what we are seeing in the détente between China and the United States is a continuation of the doctrine of containment by other means. A hostile China, backed by the United States, menaces the enormous 4500-mile border between the U.S.S.R. and the People's Republic, ties down large numbers of Russian troops and weapons, and imposes a large drain on the resources of the U.S.S.R.

This is more than mere supposition. In February, 1979, Harold Brown, Secretary of Defense, stated: "The growing Soviet and Chinese military capacities in East Asia are largely directed against each other. Their dispute has reduced drastically the probability that we will have to fight a war in Asia against China, or against the Soviet Union and China.

We no longer plan forces on the assumption of a possible ground war in China."

This is not to suggest that the United States is playing a malevolent game with China or the U.S.S.R., but simply to recognize that, without wishing to go to war, competing nations will try to keep their opponents in a state of relative weakness. In Europe, where this strategy was employed for centuries and brought to a fine art by Britain, it was known as "the balance of power." Whatever may be said against it, it is certainly preferable to a nuclear balance of terror.

Furthermore, whatever the blunders of its foreign policy since World War II, America is hardly responsible for the hostility between Russia and China. Indeed her policies up to 1972 might have been calculated to drive China into Russia's arms. But the United States-China détente has an additional bonus for America in that it helps to thwart Russia's ambitions in the Third World.

To understand this, and to understand China's global strategy, consider an address given to the United Nations Assembly, in April 1974, by Vice-Premier Teng Hsiao-ping. In this important statement Teng made it clear that to China, the world was composed of three camps. The two superpowers, the United States and the U.S.S.R. composed the First World. The other developed nations (such as Britain, Germany, and France) made up the Second World. The other countries made up the Third World. China, he said, was a socialist country of the Third World. In other words, the previous categories of thinking about the political structure of the world are obsolete. The old "blocs" of socialist states confronting capitalist states no longer exist. Instead, the countries of the Second and Third Worlds have more in common with each other than they have with the superpowers, and countries of the Third World, whether socialist or not, are natural allies. If this theory is correct, then, by virtue of its size alone, China is the natural leader of the Third World, and the U.S.S.R., whatever its protestations of disinterested friendship, can be characterized as as much an exploiter of the underdeveloped nations as the United States.

The United States, of course, can look upon this theory with satisfaction. At the least, Chinese-Soviet rivalry for leadership of the Third World can only lead to a weakening of Soviet world strategy. At best it can result in a decisive defeat for Soviet ambitions. Either way, the United States cannot lose and can derive a grim satisfaction at seeing itself joined in the pillory by the Soviets.

But this does not explain why, of the two superpowers, China should identify the U.S.S.R. as its prime enemy. First, in the long run—and the Chinese leadership is certainly thinking in terms of decades, if not of centuries—the United States will remain an opponent, and presumably the struggle between socialism and capitalism will eventually be resolved in favor of socialism. Second, Chinese tactics—formed, it should be remembered, by a half a century of war—have always been to side with the force posing the less immediate threat against the force posing the immediate one. Third, the United States has plenty to offer China. Quite apart from technical and financial aid, it alone could force the return of Taiwan, and it alone by its friendship, or at least its neutrality, could enable China to face with any confidence what she conceives to be the Soviet threat to her northern frontiers. And it is this situation which leads us to a consideration of the most important factor in this complicated international equation—China herself.

As we have seen, the overthrow of the "Gang of Four" was a victory for that wing of the Chinese Communist Party which stresses the order, discipline, and authority necessary if China is to become a powerful modern state. Undoubtedly the fall of the "Gang" was welcomed by the great majority of the Chinese people, which had had enough of the incessant demands made upon them by the radicals. But it is unlikely that the "Gang," even with the death of Mao, would have fallen so quickly without the "moderates" having the support, or at least the benevolent neutrality, of the People's Liberation Army (PLA). In this context it is significant that Teng Hsiao-ping reappeared on the national stage.

Teng, that diminutive figure who entranced the American public during his tour of the United States in 1978, is in fact a formidable and dedicated Communist of the very toughest type. After studying in France, he joined the Chinese Communist Party in 1924 and has been a member ever since. A distinguished and brave officer in the old Red Army, he made the Long March with Mao, fought against the Japanese and the Nationalists, and has been Chief of the General Staff of the PLA. Twice stripped of office—although never of his party membership—he was twice reappeared, the second time backed by Yen Chien-ying, the aging Defense Minister, and by the PLA. Teng's position as Vice-Premier is a guarantee that in the next phase of China's development the army's needs will not be ignored.

This is not to suggest that Teng is a latter-day Napoleon, riding to power on the back of the army. The "civilians" in the Chinese Communist Party have made sure of that by appointing Hua Kuo-feng the Head of the Communist Party, of the Chinese State Council (effectively the government), and of the armed forces—a unique concentration of authority in the hands of one man. Hua is also in charge of the committee responsible for the publication of the works of Mao. This appointment, surprising by Western standards, means that Hua is also in effective charge of ideology; he is the defender of the purity of the Chinese brand of Marxism. In other words, no matter how powerful the PLA might be, the civilians are still supreme and the Party still rules the Gun.

But despite this the PLA has shown its strength and importance, and we need now to ask why it chooses to demonstrate this by the rehabilitation of Teng.

The Vice-Premier is a modernizer, and he has repeatedly shown his scorn for wild, radical experiments. He and Hua between them can guarantee, as far as guarantees are possible, the development of a modern industrial base inside China. This, of course, has been official Chinese policy for many years. Chou En-lai made this clear when, in January 1975, he called for the "Four Modernizations" of agriculture, industry, science and technology, and national defense. But to establish the industrial base which will make this possible requires an efficient and motivated work force that in turn requires just that order, discipline, and authority against which the "Gang of Four" had been opposed. Teng, a hard man, is capable of driving such a program through. But this raises the second question of why the PLA should be so anxious to achieve this. The answer is that the PLA has changed its basic policies.

For twenty years the PLA had been willing enough to accept the Maoist theory of total war which, it will be remembered, consisted of the nation-in-arms submerging an invader in a human sea, with the army playing the leading—but not separate—role as guerillas. Such a war does not call for the usual equipment of a modern army, such as heavy armor, artillery, and so on. Indeed it would be impossible to secure enough bases for it, let alone for the industries to supply them. Such a war presupposes, however, that the United States would be the main enemy, and envisages land attacks on the densely populated provinces of the southeast, the Yangtze area, and the maritime provinces. But what if an enemy attacks from the north?

This is a danger that has been the concern of the Chinese for as long as China has existed. It is from the north that the Mongols and Manchus broke into China, and from there that the Japanese attacked in 1937. Even without war, China has had to struggle to maintain her grip on that vague, ill-defined area where the settled agricultural area of China proper gives way to vast steppeland and desert. Throughout history, China has gained and lost territory and population here, and there is a grain of truth in the old joke that the Great Wall was built not only to keep the Mongols out, but the Chinese in. (This refers to the fact that the Wall runs roughly along an area where the rainfall becomes insufficient to maintain regular agriculture and where the Chinese have tended to drift into nomadism—rather as if in the nineteenth century settlers west of the Missouri had tended to become Sioux or Cheyenne.) How important this area has been to the Chinese may be seen in the fact that as late as 1875, when China was being ravaged by the imperialist powers, the government, rather than spending money on its navy—a clear priority to meet the threat of the Western powers and Japan—chose instead to finance a huge expedition under Tso T'sung-t'ang in order to meet a Russian threat at Ili, 3000 miles away on the northwestern frontier.

There are three factors of strategic importance about this vast area: it is difficult to defend—Sinkiang in particular is vulnerable; it is sparsely populated, and by people whose allegiance to China is uncertain, so that an invader is not likely to be submerged by "a human sea;" and it is an area of immense mineral wealth as yet barely touched—including the vital and enormous Ta Ching oilfields on which China is largely dependent for her much needed foreign currency.

Both economically and militarily, therefore, the northern frontier is of immense importance to China. But if the U.S.S.R. was to mount even a limited serious attack there, the

PLA, as at present constituted and equipped, would be quite incapable of defending it. An estimate made by the Japanese Foreign Office in 1978 suggests that along the border the ratio of armor is three to one in favor of the U.S.S.R., and in armored troop-carriers ten to one. In air combat the Chinese would be helpless, and they have little anti-tank capability. In missiles of both intermediate and medium range, the Chinese are hopelessly outgunned, although they may have a rocket capable of reaching Moscow. In view of these figures, the Chinese superiority in manpower is meaningless, especially since, as the recent attack in Vietnam showed, the Chinese have great difficulty with the logistics of keeping their forces supplied in the field.

In view of this, it is not surprising that the PLA should see the need to modernize China's industry, and hence its own equipment, as a pressing one, and that it should be whole-heartedly behind the "moderates" such as Teng and Hua. But is such an eventuality as a war, even a limited one, between China and the U.S.S.R. conceivable? The answer must be that although improbable it is certainly possible. It should be remembered that there has been actual fighting already, and although these conflicts were small-scale border incidents, Russians and Chinese still managed to kill each other. It is, in any case, the proper task of armies to plan for any and all eventualities. We may be quite sure that the Pentagon has contingency plans for a war with Canada, for instance.

Furthermore, China has an additional problem. In the south, thousands of miles from the disputed northern frontier, is Vietnam. Armed and supported by the U.S.S.R., and with close links with the Soviet bloc in Eastern Europe (Vietnam has now joined COMECON, the communist trading organization), Vietnam is to China a running sore on her southern flank. It is unlikely that the U.S.S.R. will be in any hurry to heal the sore. For, just as it suits the United States to have Chinese troops pinning down Soviet forces in the north, so it suits the Soviets to have Vietnam pinning down Chinese forces in the south—thus putting in force a sort of Kennan doctrine of its own.

However, if it should appear that in this tangle of international power politics China is a mere dupe manipulated by the United States for its own advantage, then we should remember that China has its own diplomatic strategy to counter Russian pressure. Ex-President Nixon, a noted anti-communist, is a welcome visitor to China at any time. The Soviets see the European Economic Community as a threat to its security? Then China supports the EEC. The slightest weakness in the Soviet bloc is seen and exploited. President Tito of Yugoslavia is hailed as a world statesman and Vice-Premier Teng is happy to tour Rumania. Even Chile, a current villain of the left, is praised by the Chinese press. In fact, since it is unable to compete with the U.S.S.R. in aid to the Third World, it appears that China is making a major diplomatic effort among the Second World, of which, despite its proclamations of socialist membership of the Third World, it is not unlikely that China believes itself to be a member.

These then, I suggest, are the major factors which lie behind the present détente between China and the United States. The question remains as to the wisdom of America's policy. Here it should be stated unequivocably that not only is it good in itself, it is long overdue. It was not good for China or the world that she should be on bad terms with the United States. Furthermore, the détente can give added confidence to the Chinese government in its policy of open relations with the world, and here too, nothing but good can result. China has much to learn from the world—and the world has much to learn from China. It is also good that in this and succeeding years 30,000 young Chinese will be going abroad to study and will be able to see for themselves how the rest of the world lives (although we should not be too confident that they will draw the conclusion that other societies are better than their own). As Professor Fairbank of Harvard University has pointed out in his recent book *China Perceived*, the young Chinese who marries late, goes to work on a bike, and expects meat not too frequently, is better prepared for a future world of diminishing resources than the children of the affluent West and provides an example from which we can all learn.

And so inestimable advantages can flow from the new United States-China relationship. But one note of caution must be sounded. China must not be regarded as a joker in the pack to be played in an international poker game. The Secretary of the Communist Party of the Soviet Union, Leonid Brezhnev sounded this warning in June 1978 when he attacked those American politicians who might seek to play the "China card" against the U.S.S.R. In this Brezhnev was quite correct. Unpalatable though it might be to some, the U.S.S.R. is here to stay. It is a great power in its own right, and it is perfectly justified in carrying out policies in its national interest, as long as these are in accordance with international law. (Just as the United States has a perfect right to oppose those policies and to pursue its own policies in *its* national interest, as long as those are in accordance with international law.) If in some quarters in the United States it is felt that détente with China opens the door for a new hardline policy toward the U.S.S.R., then nothing but disaster will follow. The nations of the world have to live with each other, whether they like it or not.

In this the United States, as the strongest nation on earth, and, despite its disasters during the seventies, as the undisputed leader of the Western alliance, has a special responsibility. If America regards the present friendship between itself and China as good in itself, and if it helps the Chinese leadership to accept the realities of the world, then, global encirclement notwithstanding, consequences of incalculable value to the world will result. If not, then the world of the eighties will be even gloomier than the world of the seventies has been. Furthermore, as recent events in Iran have shown, the United States, enormously strong though it is, needs all the friends it can make in Asia*—especially when those friends are stable, reasonable, and conscious that they live in the twentieth century.

And now, although historians would rightly frown on such a question, it is natural to wonder what Mao, whom we first met in Shaoshan village in 1893, would make of the China that has emerged since his death.

* Afghanistan might appear to be a case in point. It of course lends credence to the Chinese claim that the U.S.S.R. is intent on world domination. But even if this were so it would be folly to end détente, the point of which is to solve problems sensibly. The Soviet action was taken to prop up a disintegrating client state. It will do the United States no good if, in response, it props up a ramshackle dictatorship such as Pakistan, an action which, in any case, will only antagonize India and which, incidentally, will certainly give the U.S.S.R. a powerful influence in the disaffected areas of Pakistan itself. Even suggestions that Afghanistan should be "neutralized" might not endear the United States to the Third World—including China—for they carry the assumption that the

This book is not a work of instant commentary, and there are day-to-day developments inside China, on which it would be unwise to comment. But it is a fair guess that Mao would have approved of the present policies. Except in times of crisis, Mao was always ready to accept, or make, a compromise between right and left, and to ruthlessly destroy the extremes of either wing. This is similar to the present line of the new leadership. Certainly he would be glad to see that the Party still rules the Gun, and that the Gun still supports the Party. And without question that rough shambling figure believed deeply in the historic role of China, the Kingdom at the Center of the World. He thought China had more to offer the world than the world had to offer it, and he would have rejoiced in its growing emergence as a world power. In that, if in nothing else, Mao deserved the title of Red Emperor given to him by the cold war warriors.

Not that it matters now. Mao was a hero, in the old Greek sense of the word, and, as Aneurin Bevan, the British socialist, once said of Sir Winston Churchill: "The hero's need of the people outlasts the people's need of the hero." That is to say, an hour of need comes, and a man arises to fill that need. But the hour and the need pass and new, drabber men appear, better fitted to fulfill more humdrum needs. Atlee followed Churchill, Brezhnev succeeded Khrushchev, Truman took the place of Roosevelt, Hua followed Mao.

One final word. In the summer of 1978, I was a guest at a luncheon given in England by Nobel Prize winner Dorothy Hodgkin to a party of Chinese scientists. In the course of an afternoon stroll around the Cotswold village of Ilmington, one of the Chinese observed how beautiful and well tended the village gardens were. "That is the way to live," he said. "Till your own garden, and exchange seeds with your neighbors." May it be so.

---

two superpowers are at liberty to divide the world up as it suits them. It is the opinion of this writer that the best response for the United States is to let the U.S.S.R. stew in its own juice in Afghanistan (and stew it will), while recognizing that its best defense, if defense it needs, is, rather than relying on the moral and economic idiocies of missiles and neutron bombs, to take seriously the Brandt Report on world poverty and to be ready to give aid and support itself to those governments, "left" or not, that severely need it.

Index

Index

MENTOR Biographies You'll Enjoy

☐ **GANDHI: HIS LIFE AND MESSAGE FOR THE WORLD by Louis Fischer.** The deeply moving life story of the great man who led India's struggle for freedom and preached a philosophy that influenced millions throughout the world. Index.
(#ME1623—$1.75)

☐ **NAPOLEON by Felix Markham.** Incorporating the personal letters of Empress Marie-Louise and the recently decoded diary of the man who shared Napoleon's years of exile on St. Helena, this is a pithy, succinct, and timely biography of the Emperor.
(#ME1725—$2.25)

☐ **JEFFERSON: A GREAT AMERICAN'S LIFE AND IDEAS by Saul K. Padover.** Abridged. In this stirring portrait, Professor Padover deftly reveals the personality of Thomas Jefferson, the devoted husband and father, the farmer and philosopher, as well as the crises and achievements of his brilliant career as a statesman. An absorbing, highly readable book of a great American's life and ideas.
(#MW1534—$1.50)

☐ **CHRISTOPHER COLUMBUS, MARINER by Samuel Eliot Morison.** The epic story of the great seafarer told by America's foremost naval historian. This is the breathtaking story of Christopher Columbus, the canny and skillful Genoese sailor who set out to explore the Indies and discovered the New World instead.
(#MW1662—$1.50)

☐ **GEORGE WASHINGTON: MAN AND MONUMENT by Marcus Cunliffe.** A penetrating biography of Washington that skillfully separates myth from reality. Traces, step by step, the ancestral background, the childhood, the growth, the failures and achievements of a great American.
(#ME1814—$1.75)

Buy them at your local

bookstore or use coupon

on next page for ordering.

Recommended MENTOR Reading

☐ **UNDERSTANDING ORIENTAL PHILOSOPHY by James K. Feibleman.** A comprehensive introduction to the three major schools of Oriental philosophy: Indian, Chinese, and Japanese. Each school, along with major figures and ideas, is studied individually and includes general observations by the author.   (#MJ1571—$1.95)

☐ **THE CULTURAL ECOLOGY OF CHINESE CIVILIZATION: Peasants and Elites in the Last of the Agrarian States by Leon E. Stover.** A brilliant and pioneering dissection of the Chinese past, this book explains the immense complexities and dramatic changes of China yesterday and today.
                                              (#MJ1192—$1.95)

☐ **RUSSIA AND THE WEST UNDER LENIN AND STALIN by George F. Kennan.** In a brilliant book, the former U.S. Ambassador to the Soviet Union analyzes relations between Russia and the West, from the Allied intervention in Russia in 1918 to the Cold War. He traces the diplomatic dilemmas that grew out of ignorance and mutual distrust and explains how relations can be improved in the future.
                                              (#ME1861—$2.25)

☐ **THE MIND OF ADOLF HITLER: The Secret Wartime Report by Walter C. Langer;** with a Foreword by William L. Langer; Afterword by Robert G. L. Waite. Here is the top secret psychological analysis of Hitler, just released after 29 years under wraps, that deftly fits together the facts and fantasies of Hitler's life. "Probably the best attempt ever undertaken to find out why the evil genius of the Third Reich acted the way he did."—*Chicago Tribune*   (#ME1640—$2.25)

☐ **THE PUBLIC PHILOSOPHY by Walter Lippmann.** A study of the challenges facing democratic societies by America's leading political analyst. Urges free men everywhere to take a responsible interest in government in order to preserve their liberties and defend themselves against totalitarianism.
                                              (#MW1866—$1.50)